Becoming Clairvoyant

DEVELOP YOUR PSYCHIC ABILITIES
TO SEE INTO THE FUTURE

Cassandra Eason

piatkus

PIATKUS

First published in Great Britain in 2008 by Piatkus
This paperback edition published in 2010 by Piatkus

A CIP catalogue record for this book
is available from the British Library

ISBN 978-0-7499-2936-7

Typeset in Bembo by Palimpsest Book Production Limited,
Grangemouth, Stirlingshire
Printed and bound in Great Britain by Clays Ltd, St Ives plc

Papers used by Piatkus are natural, renewable and recyclable
products sourced from well-managed forests and certified
in accordance with the rules of the Forest Stewardship Council.

Mixed Sources
Product group from well-managed
forests and other controlled sources
www.fsc.org Cert no. SGS-COC-004081
© 1996 Forest Stewardship Council
FSC

Piatkus
An imprint of
Little, Brown Book Group
100 Victoria Embankment
London EC4Y 0DY

An Hachette UK Company
www.hachette.co.uk

www.piatkus.co.uk

CONTENTS

Becoming Clairvoyant

Clairvoyance:
An Introduction

Clairvoyance, or 'clear seeing', refers to the ability to view – either externally or in the mind (with the spiritual, inner or psychic eye) – the past, the future and far beyond the physical limitations of the human eye.

Clairvoyance includes the ability to perceive energies that are of a higher level and vibration than physical matter, for example the rainbow lights called auras that surround people, animals, crystals and places. Clairvoyant abilities also make it possible for us to view, externally or in our mind's vision, the spiritual forms of nature spirits, angels and spirit guides who inhabit the astral or spiritual planes. These superimpose our own material world so we share the same space but at different levels of energy. This makes the beings of the astral plane invisible to the human eye.

Clairvoyance is an innate power we all possess both as a protective mechanism and to alert us to possibilities that have not yet appeared in everyday life and which cannot be anticipated logically. Almost every successful business person has a finely tuned intuitive/clairvoyant sense to know when to hold back and when to leap in and so, above all else, clairvoyance is a useful everyday skill.

Thousands of years ago, and still today in those few societies that practise an unbroken tradition of hunter–gathering, nomadic hunters were able to tune in telepathically to where the herds were or locate safe caves en route to their destination. Children are natural clairvoyants, as are mothers whose intuition kicks into overdrive when an infant is tiny and helpless. Indeed, mothers may still be experiencing their children's problems and fears telepathically when those children become parents themselves.

But in the modern world, natural psychic instincts become blunted because of over-reliance on technology, on what can be demonstrated scientifically or materially, and on experts to guide us to right action and interpret what we are thinking in almost every area of life.

DEFINING CLAIRVOYANCE

Though clear, or psychic, seeing is at the heart of clairvoyance, the term also includes not just *seeing* images but all methods of psychic communication that give access to past and future worlds and information that is not accessible via the physical senses. Some mediums, for example, receive all their information about a deceased person clairaudiently. This means that words sometimes come into their mind in an unfamiliar voice belonging to the deceased person or the known voice of their spirit guide. As a result, the medium can accurately describe the deceased person to the relative who has come seeking information.

Equally, some people *sense* the presence of a ghost, an ability called clairsentience, and know intuitively a great deal of information about the ghost's appearance and life history (which can be verified) even though they do not *see* the ghost, except perhaps in their mind's eye. Therefore, opening all these channels and exploring methods, as well as developing psychic vision or clairvoyance in the more limited definition, will be an integral part of the course.

Some new practitioners begin by receiving clairvoyant information through one of these related senses and then progress to actually seeing figures from the past, or ghosts, externally using clairvoyant vision. But for others who are equally gifted, these alternative and just as valuable clairvoyant channels will always dominate even when using visually rich clairvoyant stimuli such as tarot cards.

A COURSE IN CLAIRVOYANCE

Many people want to learn clairvoyance but, unlike taking a course in motor mechanics or landscape painting, there are few places you can go to take lessons. There is a shortage of accessible teaching material and teachers, and the subject can attract a mystique that makes it seem beyond ordinary mortals.

Clairvoyance can be developed by anyone, given practice, but some will find this easier and may, as with any skill, such as piano-playing, reach different standards. But everyone can attain a standard good enough to use clairvoyance by following the methods given in this book.

I teach and write about clairvoyance and related subjects in different venues and at different levels, running courses for groups including business people and experienced mediums who want to update and add new skills to their consultations. However, I have always wanted to create a multi-level course that can easily be followed at home by a beginner who wishes to develop their clairvoyant powers, and those seeking to progress further to work professionally on the circuit of psychic festivals, private consultations and the media. I also wanted to write a teaching resource that could be used as a basis for creating individual and group activities and as a part of a business training programme.

Above all, I wanted to create a DIY course for individuals who may never want to practise psychic skills as such but use clairvoyance in daily life for making the right decisions rapidly, avoiding pitfalls and seizing opportunities. This book is different from my previous books on psychic development as it will take the form of a structured graded course divided into twelve modules, containing learning material and a follow-up activity/test for each section. Each module will also offer further in-depth work, activities and research for more advanced students and professionals. You may like to read my *Complete Guide to Psychic Development* and *10 Steps to Psychic Power* as supplementary material and for further suggestions for practice at all levels.

DEFINITIONS AND EXAMPLES OF NATURALLY OCCURRING CLAIRVOYANCE

I have listed a few naturally occurring spontaneous psychic experiences from thousands I have collected over more than twenty years. Some adults may only have a significant clairvoyant experience when a family member is in danger, but for others psychic awareness is a regular part of life.

Sometimes people consult me because they are worried by frequent but randomly occurring clairvoyant experiences that manifest as disturbing premonitions, often in dreams, for example of a train or plane crash, with few details. When the disaster occurs the dreamer may be left feeling illogically responsible for not being able to prevent the disaster. Equally, ghostly figures may begin to appear, usually at night, bringing messages for people the recipient does not know. All these are signals that an individual's clairvoyant powers are emerging and need to be developed in order to bring them under control. Psychic development prevents these disturbing flashes of psychic energy and also teaches you how to close down your energies at night or when you are feeling tired or stressed. Often this surge of psychic power can be triggered by a crisis or significant change, whether it's childbirth, a divorce, a bereavement, financial change, or in older women by the menopause and in older men by a mid-life crisis.

Spontaneously occurring clairvoyance can take many forms from visions in dreams or a sudden image in the mind, to a strong sudden urge to change a pattern of everyday behaviour or act seemingly irrationally. This sudden change usually averts a disaster that would have occurred if the person had not been alerted psychically.

✧ Michelle from Liverpool had a sudden desire to hold her sleeping baby in her arms during her older daughter's assembly rather than leaving the baby as she usually did in her pram at the other end of the classroom. The ceiling collapsed over the baby's pram and a huge piece of masonry landed where the baby should have been.

✧ Neville moved into an apartment in an old converted house in London. On the first night he heard a woman's voice in his room asking, 'Are you awake, Miss Rees Davis?' When he looked, the corridor was deserted and the house silent. Curious, Neville visited the public library and discovered there had been a person called Miss Rees Davis who had owned the house in 1912.

✧ Mike from Essex was in a nature reserve and on two separate occasions saw a small fairy comparable to the size of a squirrel hovering in front of a tree about two metres in front of him, a long-haired female with four wings.

✧ Miranda from the Isle of Wight put a pot of pasta to cook on the electric stove and walked out of the kitchen. She was alone in the house. Instantly she felt herself being turned round by unseen but friendly hands. Miranda had switched on the wrong ring and the one that was lit was dangerously close to a tea towel hanging near the stove. Miranda knew it was her late grandmother who had helped her many times and had died twenty-five years before she was born.

✧ When Belinda from London was eight years old and at a boarding school for asthmatics she saw a boy sitting at the end of her bed, smiling. She screamed and woke everyone up but the head-mistress told her it was her imagination. Years later Belinda returned to the school and the former headmistress told her a young boy had died in the dormitory two years before her vision. Belinda was able to identify the boy she had seen from an old school photograph. The headmistress said she knew Belinda had seen the ghost but did not want to frighten her.

✧ When Adam from Sunderland was three he pointed to a spot in front of a bridge, saying he had died there in a plane crash. He said he had crashed on purpose. Sunderland Air Museum confirmed a British plane crashed there during the Second World War and the only person who had been killed was the pilot, saving the crew. Adam identified himself from boyhood photos of the pilot.

✧ Vera, who lives in New Zealand and is in her fifties, suddenly stopped washing the dishes and told her husband they must go at once to her mother's house on the other side of the city. Her elderly father came to the door in a total panic as Vera's seventy-five-year-old mother had fallen and broken her leg badly. Vera's father had not known what to do and had not even phoned for an ambulance.

✧ James from Oxford described how when the phone rang one morning, his wife said, 'Oh, it's Susan phoning from Heathrow Airport.' Susan was their bridesmaid twenty years before who they had not seen for many years as she was living in Nairobi. But she had suddenly returned to England without telling anyone and was indeed phoning from the airport to ask if she could stay.

✧ David, a priest from Birmingham, dreamed that a car came out of a field and smashed into his family car. The next day he and his family unexpectedly made a car journey and he identified the place the accident had occurred in the dream. Seconds later a car came hurtling out of the field. David swerved into the ditch and the family were saved.

These stories are just a few examples of how many people can show extraordinary powers of clairvoyance amidst their otherwise normal lives.

WORKING THROUGH THE COURSE MATERIAL

You should aim to spend between a week and a month on each section, depending on the hours you are able to devote. Try to develop at least four areas of expertise in more detail from the twelve parts using the suggested activities. If you have a sticking point in the course, having done the basic exercises, leave the topic and go back to it later when your overall clairvoyant abilities have increased. The follow-up activities and extra research may take much longer and you should think of the course not as an only-read but as a basic structure for your ongoing work. Clairvoyance is a profession where age is a distinct advantage but no matter what age you start learning it is a lifetime journey. For example, if you are relatively new to tarot reading, it will take months to perfect all the card meanings and I have suggested books and ways you can develop your tarot reading expertise as far as you choose. However, even with the tarot you can, after a few weeks, be proficient enough to try your skills on others, by using a highly illustrated pack for guidance and focusing on the visual card meanings. The key to success in any new psychic skill is to keep practising, first on friends and family and then progress to more distant acquaintances. You can even give yourself a quick morning-reading about the day ahead and note the accuracy of results.

Once a few people know you are psychic, word gets round and at every party or social gathering people will ask your advice. If you are an experienced psychic you can add the new skills to your existing practice as an extra while you are perfecting the techniques. I used to give free rune readings as part of a wider consultation until I felt confident that I was proficient.

If you want to become generally more tuned in an intuitive way, rather than studying clairvoyance in a structured way, the course can form an ongoing resource and after reading chapters one, two, and three you can decide which topics to explore and in what order.

ONE

Understanding the Basics of Clairvoyance

LEVELS OF CLAIRVOYANCE

Even if you are a relative beginner to the psychic arts you may be surprised at how accurate you rapidly become. The fact you are reading this book would suggest that you are open to developing your psychic powers, or if you are experienced in clairvoyance it suggests that you want to extend your gifts further in alternative, additional ways, or maybe get back your earlier enthusiasm.

Novice or expert, you are most likely to be someone who from childhood has always anticipated events and read people's deeper intentions on first meeting them. You may, over the years, have regularly seen and communicated with ghosts, angels or nature essences, and perhaps travelled in your mind or experienced what feel like out-of-body sensations to other lands and times. Many mediums open up to the spirits after a personal bereavement and sometimes the deceased relative may act as their spirit guide in the early stages of learning.

ORGANISING YOUR CLAIRVOYANT WORK

Read the material in the following teaching modules. Even if you are already expert in an area being described try the basic exercises, especially those involving nature or natural stimuli as these are rooted in clairvoyant practices established long before recorded history and can open new psychic channels. Then try the more complicated exercises until you feel that you are struggling and blocking yourself through anxiety. Exercises should always seem slightly hard, but not stressful. If you are struggling try some of the suggested activities and areas of research at the end of each chapter and then return to the more difficult exercises later in the course. The more you practise, the more accurate you become and the more accurate you become, the more you trust your psychic judgement and so access even deeper levels of awareness.

COULD YOU BECOME A PROFESSIONAL?

In theory yes, though this is an overcrowded profession. In later chapters I have suggested ways you can make the transition to earning a living through your psychic gifts, as a number of people I have taught have gone on to do. Clairvoyance is not an easy profession nor initially well paid but it is immensely rewarding to see a person you have helped become confident and turn their life around.

Whether you will become a successful full-time professional depends partly on how hard you are prepared to work, not just developing your skills but being prepared to travel to where opportunities are. For professional success, your people skills are almost as important as your clairvoyant gifts, and that includes being tolerant of human weakness.

Another requirement for a professional is being able to obtain clairvoyant information in less than ideal circumstances. For example, a crowded psychic fair is a hard but valuable teaching ground for would-be professionals as is a cramped rented consulting room in the centre of a busy town with traffic roaring by. I have had to compete against badly played didgeridoos, troupes of Native North

American dancers in full war cry, African drums at festivals, neighbours with a passion for DIY, and roadworks beneath the window of my work room.

There are many ways of using clairvoyance in a work setting, in addition to what are thought of as purely psychic consultations. You may decide to use your clairvoyant gifts as part of healing or Reiki sessions, or another therapeutic practice such as aromatherapy or massage, so you can work with your client's angels and spirit guides. Clairvoyance will also enrich psychological counselling, hypnotherapy and life-coaching work, or even form part of business training and assisting at corporate events. You may, as I did, turn to writing, lecturing and organising workshops.

If your aim is to turn professional, start in small ways, either part-time or in evenings and on weekends, while keeping your main job. Then you can gradually change the emphasis of your working life as you begin to earn a realistic wage from clairvoyance, which can take many months or longer.

Try to go and see some of the older platform mediums or the really established and not necessarily famous clairvoyants who often give talks at psychic fairs. Book a consultation with one of these tried and tested professionals and then you will see how they work and what you are aiming for.

COULD YOU BECOME FAMOUS?

For some, the ascent to fame is instant but for most it is a slow step-by-step process. Though few make the international super-star league, many others do make good livings and go on to write books and travel abroad. Most famous mediums and clairvoyants are not that much better than the unsung clairvoyants and mediums who work for a fraction of the fee. Fame partly hinges on luck – in being in the right place at the right time. However, that also means making sure you are in the right place and are known to the media when or if the unexpected break comes.

Here are some tips for using your recently honed clairvoyance in the media:

✧ Try at first for free slots on local radio or television to learn the necessary technical skills and how to fit what you do into the media format.

✧ Practise giving short, clear answers because even the most profound messages will get cut short for an advertisement break or if it is time for another guest. Forget the fifteen minutes of fame: you have a really short time to make a lasting impression so make every word count.

✧ The path to fame also involves never saying no because certainly at first you will be an on-the-day or the-day-before booking, as I have been so many times. You will get a last-minute call and you may have to travel hundreds of miles at short notice. If you are lucky you will receive expenses for your four minutes of fame – but if you do well you will be asked back.

✧ Get to the studio early and hang around after your appearance as other guests may not turn up. This is a chance to get additional air-time to show what you can do.

✧ Make sure you are always up-to-date with events nationally and locally, especially anything vaguely psychic, so if you get asked by a local paper or radio station for a comment, you'll be well prepared at a moment's notice. Likewise, learn a lot about customs and superstitions.

✧ Leave your contact details on business cards (though without gimmicks) so reporters and TV researchers will know where to get a good quote in a hurry in future.

✧ Above all, be helpful and polite to everybody as the runner getting your coffee today is the producer of tomorrow – and they do remember you.

THE ROOTS OF CLAIRVOYANCE

The first detailed records of clairvoyance in the form of scrying (seeing images in reflective surfaces) come from the magical papyri of Ancient Egypt, dated around 200 BC. Oil scrying was and still is a very popular method of clairvoyance in Egypt and throughout the Middle East.

The Egyptians and Ancient Babylonians used oil lamps for scrying. Rainwater was added to the oil during scrying when seeking the wisdom of the Sky deities such as the Sky God Horus or the Sky Mother Nut. Sea or salt water was used to invoke land deities like Geb the Earth God, and river water was used for Osiris the Father God of Rebirth and Serapis, God of Sleep. Oil lamps were also used before sleep to call a deity, especially Thoth the God of Wisdom, who would bring the answer to questions in dreams.

Most famous for clairvoyance in Egypt was the double-sided magical mirror of Hathor, goddess of joy, love, music and dance and protector of women and the family. Ordinary women kept a Hathor mirror on the family altar to answer questions about love, marriage, fertility and domestic happiness.

In Ancient Greece, though we think of the famous Oracle at Delphi, hydromancy (or water scrying) was the most common form of clairvoyance. At the spring at Taenarum it was claimed that visions of the harbours and ships of all Greece and neighbouring lands appeared. Children were frequently regarded as seers and used by adults to predict future events. Young boys under the instruction of priests would gaze into bowls of pure water lit by burning torches to see what was going to happen in the state.

In Ancient Rome, fires lit from the sacred flame of the goddess Vesta were used for divination in the home. How the hearth fire flared when offerings were made on it by a mother indicated the approval or otherwise of the household gods.

The development of scrying in Europe from the Middle Ages onwards saw the revival of the ancient arts of Greece and Rome, and mediaeval practitioners added much more formality of ritual to the process. Crystal spheres became popular in Europe during the 1400s among ceremonial magicians and alchemists, because it was believed that spirits or angels would appear in the glass and bring the required assistance or knowledge the magician desired.

The most famous prophet of this period, the French astrologer Michel Nostradamus (1503–1566), used a bowl of water or a candle to receive his visions. He is credited with successfully foretelling the rise and fall of Napoleon, the Second World War and the fall of the Berlin Wall that would happen centuries after his lifetime. His most famous detailed prophecy concerns the life of Adolf Hitler.

In England in 1581, Sir John Dee, Queen Elizabeth's astrologer, used his 'shew-stone' made of black obsidian to bring forewarning of the Spanish Armada in 1588.

A number of ancient cultures believed in both an individual and interconnected universal web of fate that was constantly being woven and rewoven according to the choices and actions of individuals and nations. The three sisters of Fate were the spinners or weavers of the web of human destiny and even that of the deities. In Christian times the Fate goddesses were downgraded to fairy godmothers in folklore, who would be present to assign a newborn his or her destiny as the earlier deities had done.

It is told in Norse myth that Yggdrasil the World Tree was fed by the Well of Wyrd, or Fate, in whose waters each morning the three Norns, the sisters of Fate, gazed to give guidance to the deities. This well contained the cosmic knowledge from when the world began and the potential for the future. The three sisters wove a web of both the fate of the world and the fate of individual beings. The first Norn, Urdhr, the oldest of the sisters, looked always backwards and talked of the past, which in Viking tradition influenced not only a person's own present and future but that of his or her descendants both genetically and in terms of wealth. The second Norn, Verdhandi, a young vibrant woman, looked straight ahead and talked of present deeds which strongly influenced the future. Skuld, the third Norn, who tore up the web as the other two created it, was closely veiled and her head was turned in the opposite direction from Urdhr. She held a scroll which had not been unrolled – of what would pass, given the intricate connection with past and present interactions.

BEYOND MEASURED CLOCK TIME TO THE WORLD OF POSSIBILITIES

By looking at the web of fate for an individual and the inter-connections with the webs of others involved in their life, it is possible for us as clairvoyants to view the possible results of choices ahead, as if these consequences were occurring in potential or eternally present time or, to put it another way, on the thought-plane of the questioner. These potential results depend not only on the choices and actions of the individual after the reading but also on the actions of those whose own fates and webs are linked to the questioner. In this way we can share with the questioner glimpses of the different likely (but not certain) consequences of alternatives: 'What if I did . . . ?' or 'What if I chose . . . ?'. This is very different from fortune-telling and is in fact fortune-making as the questioner suddenly sees options not considered and can make informed decisions.

The limitations of measured clock time, which we call real time, do not apply in clairvoyance when we enter the time frame of the eternal present. In entering this world on a client's behalf we delib-erately step or project ourselves in our minds outside the restrictions of measured clock time. But solar time, as calculated by the move-ment of the sun through the skies, has flaws of its own that we compensate for with leap years. Since the length of the day according to solar time is not the same throughout the year, mean or calcu-lated solar time was invented, based on the motion of a hypothetical sun travelling at an even rate throughout the year. The difference in the length of the twenty-four-hour day at different seasons of the year can be as much as sixteen minutes.

Even more dramatically, when the Gregorian calendar was introduced into mainland Europe in 1582, eleven days vanished from the calendar. The new calendar was not adopted in Protestant England until 1752 and so different countries were operating on a different date scale. In Sweden, for example, the calendars finally changed in 1753 when February 17 was followed by 1 March. So eternally present time is not so illogical, but is in fact the point when all time zones fuse.

THE ETHICS AND RULES OF CLAIRVOYANCE

Clairvoyance requires incredibly high standards of personal integrity. Whether you are working with friends or clients, you are dealing with personal and delicate problems. It is important to always emphasise the positive interpretation of any psychic information, suggest alternative possibilities and remind the questioner of the power they have to make changes to the future. Many people understandably want a clairvoyant to tell them what is definitely going to happen. But, of course, even the greatest clairvoyant cannot operate in total certainties and therefore to give someone what seems potentially bad news as if it were certain is to take away the free will and impetus of the questioner to make changes and avert a potential disaster. If you accept that the movement of a butterfly wing can affect energies throughout the universe then clairvoyance is always going to be affected by the free will of those connected to the questioner. These choices can sometimes lead them to act in totally impulsive ways and so change the whole equation.

What you are seeing in a reading is a kaleidoscope picture of the future at the time of the reading and by studying the patterns you can predict strong likelihoods and maybe a powerful near-certainty. But if you do give bad news you are making the negative event more likely to happen by your words. The hardest thing for a clairvoyant is to avoid the self-fulfilling prophecy whereby a client unconsciously changes their own behaviour and their interpretations of the words and actions of others according to the prophecy. So if you foretell a relationship break-up, the questioner will be giving out negative signals to their partner as a result of the reading and may look for indifference or betrayal where there currently is none (which may then make the partner more likely to go out and behave badly). Often it is better to offer an alternative. In the case of the likely break-up, suggest the client sets a time limit and tries to mend the relationship. If, after the time limit, they reassess and decide to move on, they will know they gave it their best effort. So weigh every word carefully before speaking because people may take what you say as gospel. I have written much more about this and other pitfalls to avoid on pages 124–128.

SUGGESTED ACTIVITIES

EXERCISE: OPENING YOURSELF TO CLAIRVOYANCE IN EVERYDAY LIFE

A total beginner should try at least ten of the following activities in the early stages of the course, a developing student should try at least twelve and an expert should try all of them, even in the areas they practise professionally. Assess honestly how well you did. If you succeeded in five or more out of ten as a beginner that is very good. The more experienced you are the greater initial success you should expect in all areas. Repeat these exercises about halfway through the course and your increasing psychic powers will produce even greater accuracy. Try them again at the end of the course, bearing in mind that even experienced mediums or clairvoyants will not score equally well in each area. But you will notice an overall improvement and you may have developed new areas of expertise.

✧ Visit an historic house, castle, abbey or industrial museum. Walk round without a guidebook and, where possible, touch artefacts. Sit quietly and you may be rewarded by scenes of the past or ghosts. If you encounter a ghost greet them politely, ask if they have a message for you and then say, 'Go in peace and in blessings'. Afterwards check your findings from local history resources.

✧ Spend time by still water, especially lakes and pools. Ask specific questions and, focusing on points of light on the surface, look for images as the light moves. Monitor the answers suggested by the images in the weeks ahead.

✧ Lie in long grass or among wild flowers and watch the stalks moving even if there is little wind. Half-close your eyes and let nature essences reveal their spirit forms. Look up details of what you saw or sensed in old illustrated books on nature spirits or pictures online.

✧ Go into a windy forest and ask for information about a future event. Close your eyes and listen to what the wind and the leaves are saying, as if they are voices.

✧ Switch off the incoming number display on your phone and when your phone rings, say who you think is calling (and why). Check how often you are right.

✧ Look for angel formations in a brilliant sunset or when a shaft of light penetrates the clouds during the day. Ask in your mind if the angel has a name and afterwards look up the name you were given.

✧ Ask family and friends to hide objects and then guess what is hidden.

✧ When you go to an art gallery or exhibition, memorise the details of an unfamiliar picture. Then find a blank, light-coloured wall and try to project the picture, detail by detail, as though it was on that wall.

✧ Go to antique fairs and hold different items. Close your eyes and try to imagine the item in its last setting and its original owners. You can verify this by obtaining information from the dealer and looking up the context of the item once you know its age and purpose.

❖ If you visit a new place and it feels familiar, allow your imagination to recreate images of yourself there in an earlier time. Walk round the area without a map and identify any old buildings that feel significant. Afterwards, find out about the town or region and you may discover a distant ancestor came from the area.

❖ Keep a notepad by your bed to record your dreams when you wake. If you do have a particularly vivid dream, be alert for the dream situation to occur or the main image to appear soon after the dream.

❖ At the beginning of each week, make a positive prediction of something that will happen to a family member or a global event during the week ahead.

❖ When you are in another part of the house from your pet, call them in your mind. Keep calling softly but clearly and see how long it takes the animal to respond. If you do not have a pet, call an animal or bird in a park.

❖ Think of a friend or family member you have not seen for a while and look at a photo of them or hold an item of theirs. Say, 'Call me or mail me' and picture them carrying out the action. Repeat this five more times during the same day and evening and, if with no results, the next day also.

❖ Focus on a candle flame in a room with no breeze. Concentrate on making the flame rise up or move in a chosen direction.

FURTHER RESEARCH

For your own research and the results of your exercises, start a folder on your computer or keep a notebook whose material you can transfer to a more permanent record.

❖ Using the books and websites I suggest in the appendix, explore the traditions of clairvoyance in Ancient Greece and Rome.

✧ Study the life and career of one modern media clairvoyant such as John Edwards, David Wells, Derek Acorah, Stephen O'Brien, Betty Shine or Doris Stokes and examine their path to fame.

✧ Look also at the life of one of the great traditional spiritualists such as Maurice Barbanell, who channelled the Native North American chief Silver Birch for sixty-one years until Maurice's death. Lillian Bayley was a twentieth-century trance medium who was consulted by the Queen Mother and was said to have channelled George VI shortly after his death.

TWO

Tuning Into and Developing Your Innate Clairvoyant Powers

DRAWING UP A PLAN FOR YOUR CLAIRVOYANT DEVELOPMENT

After carrying out the exercise from the previous chapter, you now have an idea of how psychically evolved you are. Define your aims and the timescale that would be ideal for you: for example, turning professional within twelve months. Look through the contents of Chapters Three to Twelve and list areas that would be helpful in furthering your current work or aims: for example, past-life work could be a useful therapeutic tool if you are already a practising professional. On the other hand you may decide to leave your future path absolutely open.

CREATING A CLAIRVOYANT WORKSPACE IN YOUR HOME FOR PERSONAL DEVELOPMENT AND CONSULTATIONS

The mark of the professional is being able to work anywhere and with a minimum of clairvoyant tools. But every clairvoyant needs a personal space to work in and materials and tools to hand to focus on spiritual exploration relatively undisturbed. Your personal space can also be your first consulting room (see pages 194–5 and 205–6). If possible, find a quiet room where you can keep your divinatory tools, crystals, candles and fragrances. Wooden garden chalets with windows are very reasonably priced and can offer both a space for personal peace and privacy and somewhere to take friends or clients for readings.

An attic, spare bedroom or basement could also be adapted. If you have to work in a room used for other purposes either put up a partition wall or use a screen or curtain. Later, you can easily rent a room if you want to turn professional.

WHAT YOU WILL NEED FOR YOUR WORKSPACE

✧ A table large enough to hold all the tools and materials you will need during a reading and a suitable cloth.

✧ Soft lighting.

✧ A white or beeswax candle in the centre of the table. At night you can illuminate the room with smaller candles as well.

✧ An incense holder on the right side of the table as you sit facing it or, if you prefer, an oil fragrance burner. Alternatively, keep fresh fragrant flowers on the table. Move the incense – or smudge as it is commonly known – off the table once you have empowered your working area.

✧ On the far side of the table set a small dish of sea salt. Change it regularly and wash the old salt away under running water.

✧ A small bowl for water, on the left of the table.

THE TOOLS AND MATERIALS OF CLAIRVOYANCE

If you do go on to practise professionally you can claim the cost of tools just like any other business.

ESSENTIAL ITEMS FOR CLAIRVOYANCE

✧ A box or cupboard for small glass or crystal bowls for scrying and holders for extra candles or incense, as well as your tarot and other divinatory tools.

✧ A separate smaller box for sea salt, oils, herbs, dried petals, candles and incense.

✧ A clear crystal pendulum in a small velvet bag kept in front of the central candle.

✧ A clear crystal quartz point. This is a small crystal with a pointed end that you hold in the hand you write with to direct energy or draw visualised circles of light. Place this in front of the pendulum also horizontal on your table.

✧ Any tarot pack with an illustrated Minor Arcana (Ace–10). My favourites are the all-purpose Rider or Universal Waite, on which most other packs are based, the mediaeval Morgan Greer or the Druid Craft tarot.

✧ Candles in a variety of colours, including white that can be substituted for any colour plus extra all purpose natural beeswax.

✧ Tea lights and holders for extra light.

✧ Essential oils such as cedarwood, chamomile, jasmine, juniper, lavender, lily, lemongrass, orange, rose and rosemary.

✧ Incense (either as sticks and cones or granular incense burned on charcoal in a heatproof dish), for example carnation, copal, Dragon's blood, frankincense, lilac, mimosa, myrrh, sandalwood, pine, violet and the all-purpose lavender and rose.

✧ Jars of dried herbs, the kind found in the spice section of supermarkets, including parsley, rosemary, sage and thyme.

ESSENTIAL ITEMS THAT CAN BE ACQUIRED LATER

✧ A crystal ball the size of a small orange or larger if you can afford it. This should be set in the centre of your table. Pick a crystal sphere with cracks or inclusions inside the clear quartz. These cracks create physical shapes such as birds, people, buildings or animals that lead your clairvoyant eye to expand and interpret them in response to a question.

✧ A set of Viking runes, the Elder Futhark. These will have twenty-four runes plus a blank. They are best in wood, clay or stone as the paint on the crystal kind tends to peel off.

✧ Twelve small tumbled crystals, more if you prefer, each round and about the size of a medium sized coin: clear quartz crystal, purple amethyst, green aventurine or jade, orange carnelian or amber, yellow citrine, red jasper or red tiger's eye, pink rose quartz, grey smoky quartz, blue lapis lazuli or sodalite, brown tiger's eye, black jet or obsidian and moonstone or selenite. A drawstring bag to keep them in.

NON-ESSENTIAL ITEMS

✧ Scented candles, especially floral fragrances.

✧ Small smudge, herbal smoke sticks in cedar, sagebrush or as a sweetgrass coil.

✧ Dried rose petals, lavender heads or chamomile flower heads.

✧ A green-ink pen, and white or cream paper.

OPENING YOUR CHAKRAS

Your chakras — the whirling rainbow-coloured spiritual energy centres within your body that empower your aura energy field — are the channel through which your psychic energies are opened and amplified by connection with the earth, nature and the cosmos. Each chakra activates a different psychic power and you may experience a sense of warm liquid or golden sunlight rising through your body as you open the energies.

Begin by picturing red light pouring up from the earth through your feet and legs and coiling round the small of your back where it is said the Kundalini – or inner energy centre, pictured as a beautiful golden-red serpent – resides. This Root chakra centre controls the physical body and your instincts, and you may feel a sudden energy surge in your feet and legs and a warm throbbing in your back and spine. The Root is the seat of your psychometric or psychic touch powers and will alert you to any danger, normal or paranormal, as well as enabling you to obtain psychic information when you handle objects or old artefacts.

Psychometry becomes even more accurate as you open the Heart chakra that rules the smaller Palm chakras. But first imagine the red light spiralling up through many small silvery energy channels through your body, to meet in a rich orange and silver sphere just below your navel. You will experience a sense of well-being similar to the feeling of being well-fed and content.

This is your Sacral chakra and is the emotional and clairsentient centre of your body where you automatically gain psychic impressions of people and places. This chakra activates the ability to walk into a place and instantly pick up from the collective aura or energy field what has happened there and the feelings of inhabitants past and present. You can also detect nature beings and power animal guides at this level of awareness.

See the red and orange lights rising together through your spiralling channels until they reach your yellow Solar Plexus, in the centre of your upper stomach. You will experience a sudden certainty and surge in confidence. This is where your psychokinetic powers reside. These powers guide your hand to pick the right tarot cards or runes and move the pendulum to answer your questions, and also allow you to call people or animals telepathically. At this level you may for the first time become aware of your spirit guides and guardian angels.

Then the energy swirls round your hands, arms and entire body to awaken your green Heart chakra situated in the middle of your chest. This chakra is the meeting place of the earth and nature energies, with cosmic light flowing down your body like a tide rushing up an estuary to mix with the river flowing into it. You may feel sudden excitement and also a sense of love and acceptance. The Heart is the seat of mediumship where you can connect with deceased relatives. You will become increasingly aware of new spirit guides who will help you in your work.

Next you may sense a bubbling in your throat as if you want to sing or laugh as the light rises into the blue Throat chakra, centred in the middle of the throat and meeting the downward flow of light. This awakens clairaudience (or psychic hearing) and also the ability to access the future, make predictions and channel messages from angels and wise spiritual ancestors. You may experience a sensation as if dark curtains have been drawn back and brilliant light is pouring into you from all directions.

This blue light rises upwards to the Brow or Third-eye chakra. The Brow chakra is filled with indigo or purple light. Here resides clairvoyance, your ability to see images of past, future and places far away. This chakra is in the centre of the brow between and above the eyes and is sometimes pictured as an extra eye.

Finally, from the centre of the hairline extending up beyond the head is the highest chakra, the Crown. This chakra is violet, merging with the gold and white of the cosmos. This level enables you to travel astrally or out of the body, and adds healing powers to your clairvoyant range. You may experience a sudden sense of a deep harmony with the whole universe.

MEDITATION AND VISUALISATION

Carry out the chakra exercise regularly as a form of meditation as well as a preparation for clairvoyance. Light a circle of the seven chakra coloured candles round you and as you sit in the candlelight you will be able to connect with each of the chakra energies in turn. Once you reach the Brow chakra level you may have a sensation of floating or flying.

For the purpose of clairvoyance we will work with meditation and visualisation together in order to relax into a light trance state. You can substitute the following exercise for the chakra work or do it as well if you have time. You can, of course, substitute any favourite methods of relaxation, breathing and visualisation and I have described several in *10 Steps to Psychic Power*.

OPENING YOUR PSYCHIC POWERS USING THE FOUR ELEMENTS

The four ancient elements – Earth, Air, Fire and Water – relate to the four natural forces and their corresponding spiritual strengths that combine to create the energy necessary for us to reach the astral or spiritual plane.

Sit or lie comfortably and close your eyes. Focus on your breathing, your inner Air, and become aware of its natural rhythm. Picture clear air flowing within as you inhale slowly and gently through your nose. Any anxiety or disharmony will flow naturally out through your nose as a wispy dark mist, or if you prefer exhale as a soft sigh through your mouth. Continue until you see and feel clear air is entering and leaving your body, with the sensation of a crisp spring morning. At this point, change your focus to your body, your inner Earth. Become aware of your bones and muscles and picture any discomfort or stiffness in them melting away. Tune into your heartbeat and visualise your internal organs working in total harmony. Again, let any discomfort flow away. Imagine your skin and hair being gently stroked and feel totally and utterly content.

Focus next on your inner Water, the blood flowing in your veins, the natural fluids in your body being regulated by hormones so that your body ebbs and flows like the sea. Finally focus on your inner Fire, the light shining from your eyes and the rainbow colours mixing and swirling around you from your aura and your chakra energy points. Picture the coloured energies moving gently like the beams from a fibre optic lamp. Finally, add Water to the Fire, then Earth and Air and let them merge with absolutely no effort from you. Say or chant softly as a continuous mantra aloud or in your mind, 'Earth my body, Water my blood, Air my breath and Fire my spirit.' Let the words fade away.

Open your eyes. You are now totally tuned in and may feel slightly spaced out.

WORKING WITH EIDETIC IMAGERY

In the previous chapter I suggested that when you visited an art gallery or exhibition you memorised the details of an unfamiliar picture on a blank, light-coloured wall and tried to project the picture, detail by detail, as though it was on that wall. The purpose of the exercise was to get your psychic senses used to working with mind images and then externalising them. Even experienced practitioners will see in far more detail by practising eidetic imaging in the following way:

✧ Choose a brightly coloured picture from a book, a painting in your home or a postcard of a painting you are familiar with.

✧ Stare at it for three minutes but do not consciously absorb the details; instead imagine them flowing into your mind like coloured rays.

✧ Take a piece of white A4 paper, stare at it for a minute, close your eyes, blink and project (push) the picture from your mind.

✧ On the paper, scribble or sketch the details in the appropriate places.

✧ Check the results and if you did not score well try with the same picture again up to three more times.

✧ Progress to even more complicated pictures until the images appear as if they were on the paper quite spontaneously and do not disappear after a few seconds but remain long enough for you to write or draw the details of the picture on the paper and *see* the images below.

EXPERIMENTING WITH PREDICTIONS, PREMONITIONS AND REMOTE VIEWING

Premonitions occur spontaneously. When you start opening up psychically or working in a more intense way, these will increase in frequency, especially in dreams, so it is important to close your chakras at night (see page 35). However, you will become more easily able to distinguish an urgent real *life warning* from a dream symbol expressing a worry. For example, a relative whom you may see drowning in a dream may be floundering under crippling debt or responsibilities, and may not have told you. One mother had a sudden vision that her baby was choking in the next room and this premonition was the real thing: 'You will know and you will go,' was what the mother told me. So if you dream of a relative drowning and you know the relative is sailing in a small boat the next day and never wears a lifejacket, this would be the time to phone and warn them so the future fate could be changed by the simple act of taking safety precautions and avoiding unnecessary risks.

INDUCING PREDICTIONS

Predictions are deliberately induced premonitions. In the previous chapter I suggested making a weekly prediction and seeing whether it came true. Initially, choose the topic of your prediction – family, work, a future sporting occasion or global event – and then carry out the following steps:

✧ Close your eyes.

✧ Breathe in through your nose while counting in your mind, *One and two and three and four.*

✧ Hold the breath, and again count in your mind, *One and two*.

✧ Breathe out through the nose, counting in your mind, *One and two and three and four*.

✧ Finally pause for the count of one and two before repeating the cycle.

✧ Repeat the cycle ten times.

✧ After the tenth cycle, let the breathing pattern become automatic and picture in your mind a screen of soft dark blue.

✧ Now picture a small pure-white dot in the centre of the screen that grows slowly into a sphere of white light that almost covers the screen, like an old-fashioned TV set being switched on in a dark room.

✧ Say, 'I wish to see an event that will occur in [name your time frame and then topic you have chosen]'.

✧ The emerging scene may be three-dimensional and may move. Your other psychic senses will kick in, perhaps through sounds, impressions or fragrances, or you may feel you are actually there (remote viewing).

✧ Wait until the image disappears, which at first might happen quickly, then allow the sphere to diminish to a dot till you only have the blue screen. Slowly open your eyes.

✧ Write down every detail you can recall, however unlikely, and you may find extra information comes to mind.

✧ If it does not work, repeat the exercise once a week.

REMOTE VIEWING

Remote viewing is the psychic ability to detect an unknown object, person or scene beyond the range of the physical eye, whether this is in another room, another building or a hundred miles away. Some people can not only see remotely, the most usual form, but hear sounds or detect fragrances.

IDENTIFYING WHAT IS HIDDEN FROM VIEW

Remote viewing is an extension of eidetic imagery. You tried remote viewing when you asked friends to hide objects from view so you could guess what they were. Here is another exercise in remote viewing:

✧ Take an unfamiliar magazine or book that contains pictures on every page, such as a book on wildlife or famous paintings.

✧ Close your eyes and choose a page number.

✧ Imagine a point of light expanding on the cover of the book like a door opening wider and wider until the chosen page is quite clearly seen. Use the blue screen and dot technique if this is more helpful and again picture the details building up from the centre.

✧ Write down or draw the details on paper as before and then open the book. If you were wildly inaccurate try this method again two or three times and if you are still getting it totally wrong return to the exercise when you are more confident.

REMOTE VIEWING WITH PEOPLE

You may find remote viewing easier when other people are involved. Follow this exercise:

✧ Ask a friend, colleague or relative who is visiting a location you do not know – from a few miles away to the other side of the world – to be your focus at the target place at a prearranged time.

✧ At the chosen time, ask them to stand near an unusual feature.

✧ Stop whatever you are doing for five minutes before the appointed time and sit quietly. Ask your subject to take a picture on a phone or digital camera of the spot and the unusual feature and note any special sounds or smells.

✧ Focus this time on the person and, looking at a blank wall, imagine the person and scene like a film projected on the wall. Note what he or she is wearing and allow the context around them to expand from the centre outwards on all sides, noting other people present and any sounds or fragrances. Trust what you feel, as even if it is a hot day the coldness you feel could be due to air conditioning if the subject is indoors.

✧ When you become more confident, tune in on people who live unpredictable lives or are travelling and note down the details and precise time you connect, even though you may not have the slightest conscious idea where they are. Check later how accurate you were.

PSYCHIC PROTECTION DURING CLAIR-VOYANCE

To protect yourself during clairvoyance, begin by lighting a central candle and asking your guardian angel and spirit guides to help and protect you. Light a small smudge or firm incense stick from the candle. Sage, cedar, lemongrass, juniper and pine are all very protect-ive. Spiral the smudge in clockwise and anticlockwise circles over the table, over tools, around the room and finally around your own body, saying softly three times, 'May all be blessed and purified and may only goodness and light enter here.' This is also a good method for protecting your table and any materials and tools you take along at a psychic fair. Alternatively, in silence pass your crystal point or the hand you write with, palm outermost and horizontal, in continuous large clockwise circles around yourself, the room, table and any tools you will be using. Picture a light sphere growing and enclosing the whole area.

If in a public place, hold your crystal point in the hand you write with, facing outwards and picture beams of light radiating from it, cleansing the space and creating a circle of protection round you and your workspace.

THE ARCHANGEL INVOCATION

If you work with mediumship, are going on a ghost watch, or are expecting an unhappy client, use the following blessing of the four archangels before you begin. It is based on an old Hebrew protective ritual and I shall describe the archangels first.

URIEL

Uriel is the archangel of transformation and melts the snows of winter with his flaming sword. Picture Uriel robed in rich burnished gold and ruby red with a bright flame-like halo. Uriel's ray is dark red or indigo.
Direction: North, or directly ahead of you.

RAPHAEL

Raphael is the archangel of healing and travellers. He wears the colours of early morning sunlight. Raphael's ray is green or yellow.
Direction: East, or to your right as you look straight ahead.

MICHAEL

Michael is archangel of the Sun and one of the chief dragon-slaying angels. Imagine Michael with golden wings in red and gold armour with a sword, shield and carrying the scales of justice, or a white banner with a red cross. Michael's ray is gold or white.

Direction: South or directly behind you.

GABRIEL

Gabriel is archangel of the Moon who carries God's messages. Picture him in silver or clothed in a blue robe of stars and a crescent moon for his halo. Gabriel's ray is blue or silver.

Direction: West, or to your left as you look ahead.

THE ARCHANGEL INVOCATION OR CALLING

To call the archangels, carry out the following:

✧ Light the central candle on your table.

✧ Stand in front of the table facing symbolic north (directly ahead of you) and say, 'Before me stands Uriel.'

✧ Then turn to face the symbolic east (or to your right) and say, 'On my right hand, Raphael.'

✧ Turn to face symbolic south (so your back is to the table) and say, 'Michael protects me.'

✧ Finally, face directly ahead again and then turn to the symbolic west (or your left-hand side as you face symbolic north) and say, 'And Gabriel enfolds me.'

✧ Face symbolic north once more and raise your arms high and wide, saying, 'The circle of light encloses me.'

✧ Look upwards and say, 'And above me is the shining star.'

✧ As you say each line, picture rays from each archangel forming a circle of light round you and, above, a six-rayed star shimmering light in all directions.

✧ If you are in a public place you can picture the archangels and the rays of light and say the words in your mind without moving.

CLOSING DOWN YOUR ENERGIES AFTER CLAIRVOYANCE

At the end of clairvoyance, it is important to close down your energies in the following way:

✧ Firstly, cleanse your tools by passing your crystal point or your hand nine times anticlockwise over them, the table and around yourself to remove any absorbed energies.

✧ Wash the crystal or your hand, whichever was used, under running water.

✧ Then close down your energy centres by passing the hand you do not write with, palm horizontal and facing inwards, over each chakra centre. Begin with the Crown in the centre of the hairline and move down in a straight vertical line through the Brow, Throat, Heart, Solar Plexus and Sacral.

✧ When you reach your upper thigh level point both hands downwards, palms innermost and fingertips extended about three centimetres away from your skin.

✧ See the Kundalini serpent re-coiling at the base of your spine and any remaining energy draining from your Root chakra back into Mother Earth.

✧ At each of the seven main chakras imagine a deep-blue curtain falling over them.

✧ Smudge round your space if you have been working with others or blow out the candle and say, 'Blessings be on all.'

✧ Have something to eat and drink and sit down for a few minutes, especially if you are about to travel home.

CONTACTING YOUR ANGELS AND SPIRIT GUIDES TO HELP YOU

We each have a guardian angel who is with us all our lives and spirit guides who come in and out of our lives at various times. Angels have never lived on earth whereas our spirit guardians are people who after death have chosen to act as spiritual guardians to the living. You may have a beloved deceased grandmother you feel close to or, if you work in healing, perhaps an herbalist or healer from an ancient tradition who has chosen to help you.

As you progress you may be aware of other spirit guides moving closer. Almost every medium has a special guide who identifies themselves either during sleep, meditation or clairvoyant work. Your guardian angel will also protect you during clairvoyance and you may sense a shimmering of light around you when they are near. Healers or experienced clairvoyants may have other helping angels. You can contact angels and guides through the method below if you want to learn more about them.

TO CONNECT WITH YOUR CLAIRVOYANT SPIRIT GUIDE

✧ Light a white candle and from it either frankincense, sandalwood or myrrh incense.

✧ Cast protection around yourself using your clear crystal pendulum to draw three circles of light. Do this by turning in a circle three times while holding the pendulum in the hand you write with.

As you move, imagine the three circles of light radiating from the pendulum at waist height, joining into a single band of light rising and enclosing you in a sphere of white light.

✧ Ask that only goodness and light may enter.

✧ Still holding your crystal pendulum in the hand you write with, ask, as you look into the flame, if your spirit guardians, or an angel if you prefer, helping you will allow you to see them. You may see a clear image in your mind, or haloed round the flame, of a spirit guide or angel.

✧ The pendulum will begin to vibrate and spiral.

✧ Put your other hand like a cup round the pendulum but do not touch it.

✧ Ask any question you wish about the identity of your guardian. Transfer the pendulum to the other hand, pick up your green-ink pen and begin to write. Continue writing till you feel there is no more to come.

✧ Ask another question and continue until you feel the energies fading.

✧ Give thanks, blow out the candle and sit in soft lamplight, reading what you have transmitted.

FOLLOW-UP ACTIVITIES AND RESEARCH

✧ Repeat the four elements exercise but this time at each stage insert images of natural elemental phenomena, such as the four winds for Air, a forest for Earth, lightning or the sun for Fire, and the sea or a waterfall for Water. Feel those powers entering you.

✧ When you are ready, add a third stage where, as each natural element is introduced, you call its particular guardian and ask if there is a message from the Earth, Air and so on. Each time you do this the elemental guardian, who may be a nature deva (being of light) or an angel of nature, will offer you more guidance.

✧ Practise meditation or just relaxation, using the physical senses to awaken the corresponding psychic senses, for example clairaudience which is an extension of physical sound. For clairaudience play a Buddhist or Gregorian chant CD or sit by a flowing water feature. For clairsentience, burn incense or oils in a darkened room. During both of these close your eyes. To awaken clairvoyance focus on a single candle flame or your crystal ball in bright sunlight or moonlight.

✧ Finally, choose a single item of natural beauty (a flowering plant, a large shell or a wooden statue) and hold it for psychometry. Do nothing, say nothing and just experience the sensations.

THREE

Clairvoyance in the Everyday World

Though we associate clairvoyance with darkened rooms, candles and polished crystals, it is actually rooted in nature. For beginners or experienced clairvoyants, practising the art outdoors reconnects them with the wisdom of the old ways and with people of distant lands and cultures who, like us, gazed into deep unmoving lakes in the moonlight or threw herbs on bonfires and watched how the flames rose up as if in answer. At any level of development, working with natural phenomena is primarily a personal art or one to share with friends and family. However, if you do work as a spiritual teacher you can, as I often do, take groups outdoors, whether into a local park in a city centre or the countryside. You can adapt any of the following methods for indoor use also.

HYDROMANCY OR WATER DIVINATION

The Ancient Greeks gazed into natural springs, at where the bubbling water emerged from the ground and also the deep pool formed by the spring, to obtain foreknowledge on both state and personal matters. The ancient port of Taenarum was believed to contain one of the mouths leading to the Underworld and had a sacred spring.

It was claimed that this spring revealed visions of the harbours and ships of all of Greece and neighbouring lands. This was obviously a great bonus to sailors and generals planning expeditions or raids. However, it is told that one day a woman washed dirty clothes in the water and the spring lost its powers.

In Rome, fountains were used to perceive figures and scenes, using the changing shades and movement of the cascading water. The fountains of Palicorus in Sicily became well known for unmasking wrongdoers; if a guilty person denied their crime the waters would bubble and reveal the evil deed for all to see.

Water scrying is a good prelude to working with mirrors as similar techniques are involved.

WORKING WITH WATER: STILL AND RUNNING

Before beginning, spend time outdoors at different times of day and in different weather conditions (such as wind, rain or brilliant sun or moonlight) near as many kinds of water – still and flowing, fresh and salt. Watch the changing patterns of light and shadow on the surface and note the various sounds and sensations you experience.

Also try gazing deep below the surface either from a boat or while swimming or paddling. Look down into a lake, the sea or an open air swimming pool. The more you are attuned to the water the more your water scrying will improve. The same technique of merging mentally with whatever your form of divination will make your readings flow without conscious effort. You don't need to use special psychic protection except to ask the guardians of the waters, however you picture them, for their permission and blessing.

HYDROMANCY IN ACTION

✧ Ask before beginning to gaze into the water that you may be shown what is of relevance to you. This can be more effective than asking specific questions.

✧ Relax totally. You may feel the boundaries of your energy field soften and merge with the water.

✧ Do not expect to see clear scenes as though peering through a window. Images for water scrying are more like those seen through a car windscreen on a rainy day without the wipers on, where suddenly the splashes clear to give a momentary picture and then the water closes in again.

✧ As you gaze into the water, focus on a single area of light or shadow and picture the water collecting like those raindrops building up on a windscreen, blurring and then momentarily clearing. Try this several times without worrying about what the images are or mean. You have to be quick as the image disappears rapidly, though in time you will become sufficiently attuned to hold the image for longer.

✧ Then watch as up to six images may one after the other appear to bubble up, disperse, collect again and then it will seem as if the energy or actual light moves away. At the same time you will become more aware of your boundaries returning.

✧ Drop a gold coin, an earring or crystal into the waters afterwards in thanks and spend time close to the water if you can and more insights may come.

DEVELOPING THE ART

It is easiest to begin water scrying with slow-moving water. Stir a pool with a nearby fallen branch, traditionally one of the water trees such as willow, rowan or alder, or cast three stones one after the other, then three more followed by three more again, one after the other. Read the centre of the ripples. If you can stand high above the pool on raised ground, or use a deep wishing well, the ripple images are clearer. Another ancient practice from Europe and the West Country is to collect seawater in a deep bowl, set the bowl on the shore and drop in nine small shells one after the other, then read the ripples. Gaze into the bowl and if you are not seeing anything, swirl the bowl as you gaze into it.

A fountain will also cast pictures, especially if you watch the kind that has bubble-domes of water and the sun is shining on it. Fountains that change colour at night through coloured lights are also excellent for scrying. As you become more confident, work with still lakes or pools, especially in sun or moonlight and with overhanging trees nearby. In a city, work with a canal illuminated by reflected lights from buildings and the embankment.

CLOUD SCRYING

Cloud scrying was one of the main forms of divination used by the Celtic Druid priests and priestesses who revered the sky along with the earth and sea. The Romans considered clouds to be prophetic. The Christian Emperor Constantine was marching against the army of Maxentius in Rome when he and his entire army saw a shining cross of light in the clouds and the words 'By This Sign Conquer'. As a result, it is said, he won the battle though his army was far outnumbered.

Cloud scrying is another activity you can practise with groups if you are running psychic courses. It is an important prelude to crystal-ball scrying where some practitioners actually see coloured clouds within the ball. If you are struggling with clairvoyance, time spent cloud watching is often all you need to tune into visual imaging.

HOW TO SCRY WITH CLOUDS

Almost every kind of cloudy sky, except for a blanket grey or a stippled sky with small bands of white markings often called a mackerel sky, is suitable and you can view the clouds either by looking up from an open space with a wide horizon or from above on a plane journey. As with all nature scrying, ask for the blessing and protection of the land guardians and if you sense an unfriendly atmosphere do not stay there.

Spend time cloud watching in different weathers and when the clouds are moving at different speeds. Identify shapes of animals, birds and figures and then see how those clouds moving closely together may be related, for example a man with a sword chasing another figure. Start weaving stories: why is the man with the sword chasing the other? What does the scenario mean to you: did you imagine yourself to be the pursuer or the pursued? Persevere with this fun activity as it will open connections between the external images and deep psychic significance. On a plane journey, book a window seat and look down through the cloud breaks on to the shadows cast on the land or sea.

Once the images you perceive in clouds are giving insight into your life, you can ask a question about the future. But this time, rather than reading each cloud or group of clouds, watch the cloud images pass until one seems touched with light or stands out. Identify the outline shape or shapes. As the cloud moves, your clairvoyant mind will fill in the details and begin to form a scenario or story. Wait for your next significant cloud image and see how this relates. Usually you will see three significant images representing an ongoing story, the resolution of which is in the third cloud image. If you prefer, identify the first cloud as the present and the alternatives, the second as the short-term future and the last as the longer-term future. When you have finished, thank the guardians of the place and bury a small coin in the earth. Linger a while as further insights may come.

SKY SCRYING

The Babylonians, Ancient Egyptians, Greeks and Romans identi-fied constellations or groups of stars as figures or animals. Taurus, for example, was associated in Egypt with the prophetic Bull of Memphis, and in Graeco-Roman astrology with the white Bull whose form Zeus assumed when he carried away the Phoenician noblewoman Europa to Crete. By a similar creative spiritual process, you can identify your own animals, people and scenes in clusters of stars that, according to the shapes your mind perceives, will relate to issues you wish to resolve.

If at all possible, work away from street lights and light pollution, but do not be deterred by less than ideal settings. You may experience an out-of-body sensation where you feel you are floating – this is the original form of astral projection (see page 139–143). Star work is an excellent prelude for clairvoyance involving other dimensions, especially angel or spirit guide work and mediumship.

HOW TO SCRY WITH STARS

✧ Lie flat or sit comfortably and look ahead at the stars on an open horizon.

✧ Breathe gently and regularly. A particularly bright cluster will become a distinctly recognisable shape.

✧ Stare at the chosen cluster until the separate stars blur. Close your eyes and when you open them blink and you will receive sudden insight into something that has been eluding you, or a totally unexpected path ahead. This first image will lead into a rapid succession of bright light-images as the original shape changes.

✧ The chosen cluster shape will eventually blur and fade. Watch the stars until you feel your concentration waning. Other ideas, words or pictures may add information as clusters form and reform.

WORKING WITH EARTH, SAND AND STONE

Natural materials such as earth, sand and stone are among the oldest clairvoyant systems on Earth and rely on our psychometric or psychic touch to transmit wisdom through the actual physical action of touch. Psychometry is a vital tool for future ghost work and mediumship as well as clairvoyance. We will develop this system with crystals on pages 71–73.

Just as skilled hunters could read the tracks of animals, so the early shamans and healers made predictions from patterns made in sand, and often added sets of symbolically significant bones or stones.

SAND DIVINATION

✧ Use a children's sandpit or a large tray of sand, or mark an area on a beach or lakeside about a metre square with a heap of sand at the centre.

✧ Spend time running your fingers through the sand, making heaps and patterns so you enter a light trance-state.

✧ Ask a question, close your eyes and allow your hands to create sand formations, shapes and patterns. Then using a stick, preferably found close to where you are working, trace lines and spirals in the formations by allowing your hand to take independent control.

✧ Open your eyes, stare at the area and interpret the scene that instantly suggests itself, before your analytical mind intrudes.

✧ Then, through half-closed eyes, view the separate areas and allow information to emerge.

WORKING WITH STONES IN EITHER EARTH OR SAND

An ancient form of earth divination is African geomancy. It offers a structure to help you make the transition from scrying to more formal systems of clairvoyance. The system spread via Arabia to Europe during the early Middle Ages where a more sophisticated system evolved, based on a grid formation and specific figures formed by patterns of dots. Each formation is given a Latin name, but each formation is remarkably simple.

This method can be adapted for psychic fairs or private

consultations by using a small tray of earth and small crystals, as can basic sand divination. In both cases you interpret the images created by the client. Work on a smooth patch of either soil or sand (or snow in winter) and draw a twelve-square grid (see below). Draw your grid three boxes wide by four deep. You can make the grid large enough to walk round if you are working outside.

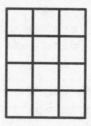

You need eight round dark brown pebbles or dark brown earth crystals, such as fossilised wood or smoky quartz, to mark the dot formations. Keep these in a drawstring bag.

Creating a Divinatory Figure on the Grid

✧ As with all divination, you need to make an apparently random selection, in this case four either odd or even numbers marked on the grid with your pebbles, to make up one of the symbols I have described below. You will also need a single stone with a single dot on one side for odd numbers and two stones on the other side to indicate even numbers.

✧ Ask a question about the future (up to six months ahead) concerning you or a named person.

✧ Toss your single number stone in the air to determine if your first number is odd or even. An even number is represented as two stones on the grid: one stone in each of the outside columns. An odd number is represented by a single stone in the middle column. Mark the grid by putting the stones, either odd (one) or even (two), into the relevant column of the top row.

✧ Throw the numbers stone three more times until each row has one or more pebbles.

✧ Close your eyes and allow the basic template meanings listed below to expand in words, images and impressions.

✧ For a complex matter, remove the stones and repeat the divination for a second or third time.

The Sixteen Stone Formations

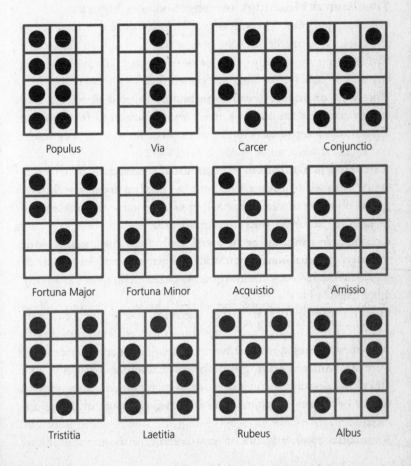

Populus   Via   Carcer   Conjunctio

Fortuna Major   Fortuna Minor   Acquistio   Amissio

Tristitia   Laetitia   Rubeus   Albus

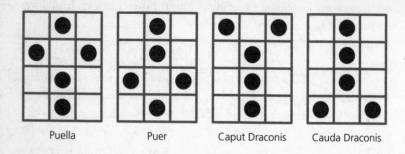

Puella   Puer   Caput Draconis   Cauda Draconis

Traditional Meanings for the Sixteen Figures

Populus (people): The will of the majority; dealing with a group of people at work or socially. Justice, the law and officialdom; it advises going along with others or the need to go through existing channels to achieve an aim. Successful social events.

Via (way or road): Travel opportunities or well aspected travel; the life path and the need to avoid being sidetracked from goals; a solution to a long-standing problem; the need for independent action and focusing on a single goal.

Carcer (prison): Delays, frustrations and limitations, whether in family, personal or financial matters; the need to actively seek ways round obstacles or fears, especially self-imposed ones; or deciding to keep the security of existing limitations.

Conjunctio (joining or union): Unity and compromise; love, togetherness and contracts; favourable partnerships of all kinds; successful legal matters and the need to increase communication with the wider world.

Fortuna Major (great good fortune): Deserved good luck, success, victory or increased status; career success and promotion; a door opening that was closed; fame and recognition; desired approval.

Fortuna Minor (lesser good fortune): Promises assistance from others and slow but sure progress; suggests favours or money owing should be called in; setting your own definition of fulfilment and success.

Acquisitio (gain): Financial gain, whether in business, property;

improvement in health; a good time for speculation, launching commercial ventures and money matters generally.

Amissio (loss): Warns of the need to avoid potential stress, critical people and no-win situations; stepping back from others' quarrels and saying no to unreasonable demands; confide only in trusted sources.

Tristitia (sadness): Do not waste regrets on what has been lost or might have been; focus on gains rather than losses; value yourself as you are and look for the light that is at the end of the tunnel.

Laetitia (joy): Happiness and fun, unexpected good luck; favours any celebration, birth, marriage, holiday, or family matter; promises joy in love and friendships, both new and established; enjoy the present rather than worrying about the future.

Rubeus (red): Warns against giving way to unwise temptations, irritability and over-indulgence of all kinds; speak and act with caution; deal with injustice in a firm but controlled manner.

Albus (white): New beginnings; new relationships; fertility; healing; positive results concerning children and young people; reconciliation and heightened creativity.

Puella (girl): The blossoming of potential, especially in sexuality, friendship and romance; less positively a desire to avoid responsibility or make difficult decisions; watch out for manipulative people who act helpless.

Puer (boy): Avoid unnecessary risk-taking or impulsive behaviour; avoid giving up on a relationship or situation because it is temporarily unexciting or unfulfilling rather than trying to improve it; also originality, an adventure (maybe a bit challenging) and unexpected opportunities.

Caput Draconis (head of the dragon): What is worthwhile, aiming high and initiating long-term plans; a life change or location change; working for oneself; the ultimate symbol for fulfilling dreams or going for something that seems impossible right now.

Cauda Draconis (tail of the dragon): Closing doors on what did not work or is no longer possible; avoiding repeating past mistakes; refusing to be bullied or silenced or going along with less than honest behaviour or quick fixes.

Geomancy in Practice

I first threw an even number. I put two dots or stones on the top row of the grid, one on either side.

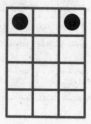

My next throw was an odd number so I put one dot in the middle column on the second row.

The third throw gave me another odd number and another single dot.

My last throw was an even number giving me two dots and the figure of Conjunctio.

Conjunctio answered my question about writing a new book that would need a lot of research in a short time frame. Conjunctio with its association with contracts was a favourable omen. But how could I collect all the necessary data in the time given? The answer was Conjunctio, to connect this time with the Internet – the ultimate connector.

WORKING WITH FIRE

Pyromancy is the name given to the art of divination by fire. The first certain evidence of hearths can be traced back 125,000 years and we can only guess the antiquity of the earliest sacred fire ceremonies where the direction of flames and their intensity were interpreted by priests and priestesses as expressing the intentions of the deities. Tibetan fire scrying invoked the spirits of the fire and also studied the direction and intensity of the flames.

For the purpose of clairvoyance, the importance of fire scrying lies in using the moving, dancing flames and the more concentrated areas of the burning embers as a backdrop for intense moving images. Working with open fires is a good prelude to candle scrying. Candle scrying is probably easier with clients, though I have successfully worked scrying with groups round open-air fires.

BEGINNING FIRE SCRYING

✧ Create a source of fire such as a bonfire, a fire lit on the shore of a lake or a beach, a domestic fire, a wood-burning stove or one created in a small incinerator, a chiminea or metal garden burner.

✧ Wood is the most natural fuel source and, especially with pine or cedar, can be fragrant.

✧ Once the fire is burning, throw a handful of salt on the fire and, indoors or out, ask the blessings of the guardians of the land on which the fire is kindled.

✧ Cast a handful of dried herbs or flowers into the fire.

✧ Look into the centre of the flames as the herbs kindle and you will see a sudden scene flash in the momentary blaze. When it dies down look at the sparks, embers and deep-red areas closer to the base of the fire in the same area and the picture will appear in more detail. You may need to keep blinking as this is very intense.

✧ The first picture reminds you clearly of what you need to know from the past to illuminate the present. Wait a minute or two after the images have faded and then cast a second lot of herbs or flower petals into the fire in the same place. This time you will see a scene that will reveal something about the present you do not know, maybe someone helpful or less than supportive, or a chance that you have overlooked.

✧ Finally cast the third lot of herbs or flowers and you will see the future with yourself in a desired but maybe unexpected way, which will hold the key to realising that future.

✧ When you have finished, leave the fire to burn out and if on a beach check tide times so the water will come in and cover the fire. Alternatively, cover the fire with earth rather than putting it out with water, and if possible bury the ashes where you lit the fire.

✧ Remember to thank the guardians and to leave everything as you found it.

READING NATURAL OMENS

For thousands of years people have interpreted the signs of nature: storms, rainbows, mists, angelic or deity-like figures seen in sunset cloud formations.

The Maoris called these omens *aitua* and believed that the ancestors and deities spoke to them through natural phenomena. For example, a short sharp shower in an otherwise blue sky was seen as *waewae tapu* (sacred footsteps) and suggested that the ancestors had drawn near and so action should be swift, whereas the God of rain in his form of Ua-Roa (Long Rain) might suggest long-term favour. Natural objects which behave in ways contrary to natural laws, for example a log floating upriver, would indicate an uphill struggle or unexpected obstacle.

Sheet lightning indicated problems stemming from human error. A low rainbow directly ahead would indicate that a projected journey might be difficult. A high-arched rainbow promised favour on any enterprise and one forming a circle assured total success and happiness.

But beyond the basic message came the clairvoyant insights, the pictures promoted by the sheet lightning, for example, that might seem to offer sudden illumination as to how a wrong course of action or direction might be corrected. Words or impressions would flesh out the basic omen.

FOLLOW-UP ACTIVITIES AND RESEARCH

✧ Use old folklore books and online resources to research the different weather and other natural omens in at least two unconnected cultures and note any common features that appear.

✧ Since clairvoyance relies on the interpretation of symbols, this is a good point to begin your own symbol system resource. Note if any particular symbols have emerged during your work in natural scrying and what their general significance is (look them up in symbol books or the numerous symbol online websites, and then what they mean in your life. Every symbol has both a universal and personal meaning. Understanding your clients' symbol systems will be a key to success so begin with your own.

✧ Go back to the omens you researched. Imagine you have created your own culture and beliefs about nature. Rough out your own omen system and add the individual entries to your symbol list.

✧ Whenever you see an unusual natural phenomenon, note what you feel and monitor any unexpected events that happen shortly afterwards.

FOUR

Developing Clairvoyance Through Traditional Scrying Methods

In the previous chapter I described ways in which the natural world amplified innate clairvoyant powers. The same natural powers can be brought indoors to enrich your personal or professional skills. Throughout this section I refer to images you will see in a crystal or mirror. These may be actual pictures of people, or scenes you can relate to. More often they are symbols similar to the kind we see in dreams. Most meanings are self-evident: for example, a baby may be an actual baby if fertility is an issue but more often refers to the eventual success of a creative venture that needs much preparation and effort.

SCRYING WITH CANDLES AND WAX

Ceroscopy is the name given to candle scrying, or seeing images in either the candle flame or its melted wax. Candle wax scrying is good for working with psychic groups or an individual client if you explain the techniques beforehand. Though I prefer to use natural products (beeswax, vegetable or palm oil candles) for clairvoyance, for wax scrying specifically, paraffin wax candles burn faster and so produce wax patterns more rapidly.

Make sure the colour goes all the way through the candle as cheaper ones are just coloured on the surface and white within. Beeswax is good for studying the flame and also interpreting the shapes formed by the melting wax running down the side of the candle. However, beeswax forms globules if dropped on paper or in water. Bayberry candles, which have an aromatic green wax, are good for wax scrying and burn very rapidly, but can be brittle.

WAX DIVINATION ON PAPER TO ANSWER QUESTIONS

This is the easiest form of wax divination, apart from the obvious risk of setting fire to the paper. It allows you to create quite complex images and add different colours that flow into one another.

You will need:

✧ Thick A4 white paper (black if you are using a white candle).

✧ A selection of candles in bright colours. Tall taper-like candles are better than squat ones. If you prefer you can use a single dark blue, green, white or purple candle.

✧ A heatproof non-absorbent surface under the paper so the wax does not soak through.

Method:

✧ Light up to four differently coloured candles. If you are working with a client they should choose two of the four and drop the wax at the same time as you do, one colour after the other on to the paper.

✧ As you light the first candle, state the purpose of the divination, which may be a specific question or area of concern, or 'whatever is right for me to know'. Ask for the protection of light (or of your special guardians), asking that the visions be pure and true and for the highest good.

✧ Take your first candle and slowly drop wax on to the paper, in spirals, circles or just drops that are close together. Then tip the paper so that the wax forms pathways.

✧ Note the image formed. Look through half-closed eyes as the image may in fact be a whole scene.

✧ Add a second colour around or on top of the original wax and tip the paper again so the image changes and now is made up of both hardened and flowing wax. Continue until you have used all the colours. If working with a single colour, repeat the process four times.

✧ The first image gives relevant information from either the recent or instant past, or maybe a past world. The second image reveals the build-up of events and influences leading to where you are now. The third image shows the changes that will result from the events and/or subsequent actions of the four weeks ahead and the final image reveals the summary of what may be possible in the months ahead given the actions or progression of events suggested in the third image.

✧ If working with a client you can ask them to define the question and what they see. After the exercise put your two interpretations together.

WAX ON WATER

Wax on water is an even more evocative method since the wax flows on the water and gives a vivid moving image followed by a static one. Speed is of the essence in this practice.

- ✧ Use a large light-coloured ceramic bowl the size of a serving dish, half-filled with water.

- ✧ This works best with at least two colours. You can hold a lighted candle in both hands if you wish.

- ✧ Drop the wax quickly over the surface of the water in spirals.

- ✧ The molten wax will swirl on the surface and may sink, giving further images as it does so, gradually hardening to make a multi-coloured image.

- ✧ The different molten images build up and flood your mind with details. Only afterwards will the meaning be clear as your mind is storing the impressions as they emerge.

- ✧ Lift the wax shape out of the water and leave it to dry. It will make a distinctive shape such as a dragon or a butterfly. If it's more abstract, liken it to an abstract sculpture.

- ✧ Hold the shape, or ask the client to do so, and without pausing for conscious thought name ten feelings, phrases or pictures evoked by the image. This really needs to be fast to avoid conscious analysis and dismissive logic.

- ✧ Wrap the shape in cloth and keep it as a talisman, or give it to the client to take home.

- ✧ Sit quietly by the light of the scrying candles. If with a client talk over the possibilities or add another form of divination. When you are ready, blow out the candles in reverse order of lighting, thanking the guardians as you do.

- ✧ Add a pinch of salt to the water and then wash the bowl out.

- ✧ Another method is to stand a wide, short pillar candle in a wide metal bowl and while the pool of wax is still molten, blow out and remove what is left of the candle. Pour some of the melted wax carefully into a large container of water and read the created images.

CANDLE FLAME SCRYING FOR CONNECTION WITH OTHER DIMENSIONS

Though candle scrying is best for private use, you can sit in a circle with a psychic group, each with a candle lit from one central candle. Go round the circle, each member giving messages from their individual flames on matters of joint or more global concern.

Candle flame scrying will connect you to your guardian angels and spirit guides, or with wise ancestors if you wish to communicate with them. As you become more experienced, you can use this method to talk mind-to-mind with them and be shown visions or images. However, unless you ask to talk with your angel, you will most likely encounter a golden candle-guardian in the flame who will bring you a message. This is a largely passive process. You may discover your candle guardian is clearest when you use a particular fragrance, so do experiment.

Success in candle scrying lies in attaining a totally relaxed state. Try first when you are sleepy and can hardly keep your eyes open. Set a broad, squat, scented candle in a rounded glass holder so that the flame casts light-patterns on the glass. You can embed the candle in ornamental sand or gravel for safety. Rose, lavender, jasmine, sandalwood and bergamot are all good divinatory fragrances. Candles containing essential oils in palm or vegetable oil are especially good as they do not give off smoke or shed wax. You can also buy smaller ready-fragranced candles set in glass containers. Candles in glass are also effective for outdoor night time scrying.

EXPERIENCING CANDLE SCRYING

✧ Work in total darkness except for the candle. Soft music in the background may help when you first begin.

✧ Half-close your eyes. Look at the flame and the light patterns, blinking when you need to. Ask that your candle guardian tell or show you what you need to know and that you will be protected by the light.

✧ Look at the area around the candle and, just as you did with the blue screen and dot technique (page 30), picture a sphere of light expanding around it so that it becomes a large circular screen.

✧ To assist this process, imagine you are gently inhaling the light around the candle, visualising that golden light entering your own aura energy field. Then exhale softly though your mouth like a sigh so you picture the golden light expanding around the candle to create a sphere within which the guardian can appear. The dark inner wick within the flame forms a doorway.

✧ Your candle guardian will stand framed in the doorway with a message or with information for you that you may hear telepathically. You may be shown images in the flame which tend to be red or orange but may be black outlines. The images almost always move and flicker even if the flame is still and tend to be two-dimensional.

✧ Look also at the reflection of the flame in the melting wax to see a double image of the flame.

✧ Make a regular time for candle scrying two or three times a week. Dedicate one session to healing when you will ask your candle guardian to heal people or animals you know, or to help places affected by suffering or a sudden disaster.

✧ When your guardian fades, blow out the candle and send the light and love to all who need it, not forgetting yourself.

SCRYING WITH CONTAINERS OF WATER, INKS AND OILS

INKS ON WATER

Ink scrying originated in the Middle East and was practised during the hour before sunset. If possible, work outdoors and experiment with different positions where the sunset will be reflected in the water. However, if you are indoors work in soft light and if necessary light small red candles behind the bowl of water. Use the following guidelines when scrying with ink on water:

◇ A large white or plain glass bowl is best to allow the ink to spread and sink quite rapidly. Images will change into others as the ink moves through the different levels of the water.

◇ Use red, blue, black or green waterproof ink, and more than one colour at once if you wish. Ordinary writing ink is fine though some New Age stores sell magical inks and these can give very clear images as the ink tends to be quite thick.

◇ Use slender, small-bristle paintbrushes or a nib pen with a wooden handle. Use separate brushes or pens for each colour. Put the open inks around the bowl.

◇ Practise dripping ink drop-by-drop on to the surface of the water. Use the ink sparingly as you can easily add more. With your free hand gently tip the bowl after adding the ink. If with a client, you can both add drops of ink simultaneously.

◇ The interpretation has to be quite rapid as the images change and subsequent images continue to form until the ink settles as a final shape at the bottom.

◇ Ink scrying is especially good for specific time-frame issues and for 'When should I . . . ?' questions.

◇ Ink scrying is also good for choosing between specific options – you can wash out the bowl between named options. If you are only considering two options have two identical smaller bowls of water side by side and add ink alternately to the two bowls to see the different options developing.

OIL SCRYING

Though oil scrying in Ancient Egypt, Greece and Rome involved a variety of techniques including hot-oil scrying, the most practical version in modern clairvoyance involves dropping cold oil on the surface of water. It is best used as a personal development technique, though you can teach it to more advanced students. It can also be a good prelude to a healing session or to centre yourself before a busy period. The most successful method involves pouring oil (such as sunflower, almond, olive or grapeseed) from a small narrow-necked bottle or flask, a drop or two at a time, onto the surface of a large, deep, white or cream ceramic bowl filled with water. You can use perfumed oils if you prefer.

Before you begin, anoint your brow with either the perfumed oil or a single drop of the oil you are scrying with. Make an eye-shape in the centre of your brow and ask that your clairvoyant sight will be open and that your guardian angel and guides will protect you on your journey.

Oil wisdom is a very profound method and works by creating a circular astral oil doorway or eye-shape or two or three oil circles as the oil floats on the surface of the water. This accesses other worlds where power animals, nature essences, spirit guides, angels, ancestors or recently deceased relatives live. You can specify the guardians you wish to encounter or ask to see whoever will be of most guidance at this time. For the best results, follow these guidelines:

✧ You need a good light source: either natural sun, moon or a semicircle of small white candles behind the bowl of water that should be just over half full.

✧ Oil scrying is very unpredictable and even if you pour only a few drops you may create two or three eye formations or circles. If you have a choice, focus on the circle or eye you feel drawn to. One is enough per session.

✧ Breathe yourself through the doorway by looking directly down into the oil with half-closed eyes, inhaling slowly and gently through the nose. As you exhale softly through the mouth, imagine you are passing through a shimmering warm curtain of liquid light that parts to let you enter.

✧ Keep focusing on the doorway, blinking when necessary, and you may become aware of your particular guardian who will help you discover whatever it is you need to know, either for yourself or for a client. The information may come suddenly to your mind or you may experience a telepathic dialogue. You may be shown images or scenes that will explain what has been puzzling or worrying you.

✧ When you sense the connection fading, focus once more on your breathing and you will become aware of the bowl and the oil circle. Thank your guardian and wash the bowl out, having added a pinch of salt.

✧ If you do want answers to more specific questions, pour the oil into one bowl of water and then tip the oily water rapidly into an empty bowl and then back again two or three times until the oil is swirling. Look at the oil formation, blink, open your eyes and you will *see* what it is you most need to know.

CRYSTAL SPHERE SCRYING

Choose a crystal ball without cloudy areas but with sufficient markings within the sphere to form rainbows and intertwined pathways. This is an excellent method to use with clients as they see instant static images and then tell you what they see, feel and hear. As you become more experienced you will see small but totally clear images moving within the ball and also the background around them. One image will change into another and then another in sequence.

TUNING INTO THE CRYSTAL BALL

✧ Polish your ball with a soft cloth, kept for the purpose, both before and after a session.

✧ Before you begin, hold the crystal ball between your palms. Picture rich green light from your Heart chakra energy centre flowing down your arms and through your hands and fingertips down into the ball. Imagine white light from the ball flowing up via the same channel to your Heart chakra. The Heart chakra is naturally attuned to all crystals.

✧ Light a candle or hold the ball up to the light source and you will feel its energy in your fingertips.

✧ Finally ask the spirit or guardian of the crystal (all spheres have one) to assist you and your guides in your work.

SEEING AND INTERPRETING IMAGES

✧ You can scry with your crystal ball outdoors in sunshine or by moonlight, or indoors in natural light or by candles after dark.

✧ Ask a specific question so that you will be shown what you most need.

✧ Hold the ball up to the light and turn it until you identify your first image.

✧ Now you are going to extract detailed information about the image to find a solution to your question. The image will represent the person or situation under question. Subsequent images will show related people and events, and the future that is possible if you act on the information you receive.

✧ An example I often use in teaching the technique is a bird. When you see the bird, ask yourself, What kind of a bird: a small one or a huge bird of prey? Is the bird soaring or nesting in a cage?

And if the latter, is the cage door open? Does the bird know the cage is open and what stops it leaving? Who or what does the bird signify? You can ask a client these questions about the images they see.

✧ Alternatively, if the client does not want to look in the ball, you can describe the image you are seeing and ask them what they feel as you describe it and how they relate to it.

DEVELOPING THE IMAGE WORK

✧ If a second image can't yet be seen then focus on the previous image or the area of the ball you saw the first image until you identify the new one. The first image may change into the second image and this new image will provide relevant information about other people known to the questioner, connected with the question. The third image will show the future.

✧ You can, either in private or professional work, add further images or further changes to the original image; the fourth relating to helpful influences, the fifth obstacles to be overcome and the sixth a longer-term view of the possibilities for the future over the next twelve months (this last image may expand into a scene).

✧ Alternatively, you can look for only three images to signify the past (what is moving out of a person's life), present factors (options that are unknown or recognised but currently exist) and the future (what is moving into the person's life).

✧ Some people see clouds in the glass and these can be read just like clouds in the sky, as described in the previous chapter. One generally follows another in rapid succession and four or five will form a sequence before the ball becomes misty inside and there is no more information.

CLAIRVOYANCE WITH MIRRORS

In both Ancient Greece and Rome, mirror scryers called *Specularii* used bronze mirrors to see into the future. Copper and silver were also used for magic mirrors. But it is from Ancient Egypt and the goddess Hathor that the most exciting concept of mirror scrying arose, where it was said it is possible to see yourself as you can become. While for some set on a destructive path this might be a warning, for many who lack confidence this is a very empowering and liberating process.

HOW TO READ MIRRORS CLAIRVOYANTLY

✧ You need a mirror large enough to see your whole face when you sit in front of it. A free-standing one is best. A swivel mirror will enable you to move it to the right angle to catch the light. Round or oval are traditionally used, especially those with silver frames.

✧ Work in daylight with sunlight casting beams on the mirror. Moonlight is best, in fact, but you can also use clear natural light. After dark, candles should be placed so you cannot see the flame within the mirror.

✧ Monday is considered the best day to practise this method of clairvoyance.

✧ Because mirror divination does take a lot of practice, it is not one suitable for consultations except for past-life work, though you can have a special mirror for clients to look into at the end of a positive session to see themselves as they could become.

✧ Make sure that the mirror is facing a blank wall, or if outdoors an open space, so that the background does not reflect in the mirror.

✧ Polish your mirror clockwise before use with a special cloth and ask that your visions may be true and beautiful, and bring goodness and hope. Ask that Mother Hathor (or your guardian angel or spirit guides) will bless and protect you.

✧ The technique whether for scrying by daylight, sunlight, moonlight or candlelight is the same. Place any candles in a semicircle behind you or along the base of the mirror.

✧ Sit so that you are at the side of the mirror so you can see into it but do not see a reflection of your face.

✧ Practise looking for images. Do not expect to see an image as clear as a normal reflection. Images may appear quite faintly sometimes as a light shimmer, at other times emerging in a shadow, maybe an outline, or a grey formation, coming together in a shape and as quickly dissolving like wisps of mist, always fleeting. On other occasions the image can move in and out of vision like the ripples clearing.

✧ What you are left with is a strong impression in your mind, often more powerful than images seen more tangibly in other forms of scrying. You might think you saw nothing clearly except that you are left with an image that was released from the reflective mirror and became very clear and vivid in your mind.

✧ If images do disappear too quickly, keep staring at the spot of light in the mirror where the image appeared and you will be able to recreate it in your mind. As you become more experienced, recall it again into the glass.

✧ Incense sticks by the mirror will swirl incense upwards, reflecting in the mirror, and help to soften the glass and make it seem more fluid.

HOW TO ASK QUESTIONS IN YOUR MIRROR

✧ Half-close your eyes and look first into the top right corner. This will tell you about the past, recent or distant, most relevant to the question or what is passing from your life. If you wait as the image fades, it may be followed by a second or even a third image as a timeline, if, for example, you have made the same mistake before and are about to make it again.

✧ Pass your hands in anticlockwise circles in front of the mirror, a few centimetres from the glass, palms vertical to the mirror and with fingers together, to clear away the past impressions.

✧ Close your eyes for a moment and open them again slowly. Focus on the centre of the mirror to see the present issue. Again you may see more than one image especially if you are being torn two ways or if hidden information is about to emerge. The first image seen in the centre may relate to what you need to let go in order to take advantage of opportunities or relationships on offer.

✧ Clear the mirror again by passing your hands in front of it in circles as before.

✧ Close your eyes again and as you open them slowly, look into the far top left of the mirror and see what is coming into your life. The first image is usually related to the step you have to take into that future. Then you will see further into the future either in a short-term timescale or perhaps several years on. You can specify a timescale before looking for the future images.

SEEING YOURSELF AS YOU COULD BECOME

✧ Finally look directly into the mirror so you can see your face and you will see yourself as you can become, given belief in yourself. This self-knowledge and increased self-esteem mean that the prophecies revealed in the images of the future are more likely to be fulfilled, because you are open to embracing new opportunities and new people.

✧ Very slowly close your eyes and open them equally slowly and you will see what is possible: the happy, fulfilled person you will become and around you the environment where you will fulfil that future.

✧ As the vision fades you will see yourself as you are now once more, but framed in light and glad that you are as you are.

✧ When you feel the connection fading, sprinkle a few drops of clear water on to the glass and polish it anticlockwise with the special cloth. Finally, anoint your four upper chakra energy centres (the centre of your hairline, the centre of your brow, your throat and both your inner wrist pulse points for your heart) with the same water.

DARK MIRROR SCRYING

Dark mirrors are gateways into other worlds and were frequently used among the Mayans and Incas who scryed in pure obsidian. I have written in detail about dark mirrors in Chapter Eleven as they are one of the most useful tools for past lives, work with ancestors, angels, spirit guides and astral travel. They are less suitable than clear mirrors for clairvoyance concerning decision-making.

FOLLOW-UP ACTIVITIES AND RESEARCH

✧ Continue working with your personal symbol system, adding new information and symbols.

✧ Reassess your clairvoyant tools and try to find items that are right for you: beautiful scrying bowls, unusual perfume oils, hand-made candles or traditional incenses. Acquire other crystal balls such as amethyst or smoke quartz that we will use in work with past lives and ancestors. Look for statues of deities that have significance for you, crystal angels to protect your working space and beautiful pictures to adorn it.

✧ If you are experienced in clairvoyance try to create the Eye of

Horus, the young sky god, in oil on the water. You may need to use your oil in an eye dropper. It is said if you look through the Eye of Horus you will *see* the symbol that will unlock other dimensions.

- ✧ Try still-water scrying in a black ceramic or smoked glass bowl, putting small candles in a semicircle behind the bowl and working in total darkness. Stare deep down into the water and this time create your own watery doorway in your mind to where is right for you.

- ✧ Finally, to develop your psychokinetic power, create in your mind a positive statement or empowerment about your life as you would like it to be, as you sit looking at the clear water. Practise in the days ahead until the image of your successful achievement appears in the water. As a bonus you will find that the empowerment begins to take effect in your life.

In the next chapter we will work with the other psychic powers that are part of clairvoyance, such as clairaudience and clairsentience, so that your clairvoyance becomes more detailed and accurate. We will test all the powers by working with twelve or more small crystals. I have listed these on page 24 – try to obtain them before reading the next chapter.

FIVE

Expanding Your Clairvoyant Powers

Since all the psychic senses are closely related, we will practise them by using crystals that draw together the different channels in a single spiritual method of divination. As a bonus you will learn an unusual divinatory art to supplement and amplify psychic consultations. Because of the limitations of space in this packed book I have only listed twelve crystals (plus alternatives). You can work with as many small crystals as you wish. Each should be round or oval, polished and of similar shape and size to a medium-sized coin. Keep them in a drawstring bag large enough to put your hand in and move them around.

I have listed the full divinatory, protective, luck-bringing and healing properties of 150 crystals in my *Illustrated Directory of Healing Crystals* if you want to work with more.

STARTING CRYSTAL DIVINATION

Select one crystal from your drawstring bag each morning, after feeling all the stones in turn and choosing the one that feels right, to tell you what you need to know about the day ahead. You are attracted to a particular stone through psychokinesis, the power of the mind to guide the hand to select apparently randomly what is needed to answer your question. This innate power is behind almost every form of divination involving the selection of a card or stone.

Hold the chosen stone between closed cupped hands (activating psychometry or psychic touch) allowing your hand chakras to channel psychic impressions via the stone. The crystal offers not only wisdom connected with the significance of the crystal itself, but also information from the universal well of wisdom or Akashic records. These repositories are believed to contain the wisdom of all times and all places including the potential future and the wisdom of angels, guides and ancestors. This information is then translated into impressions (clairsentience), pictures in your mind (clairvoyance) and words (clairaudience).

Now move through the following steps:

✧ What do you feel when you hold the crystal and think about the question or day ahead? Often the emotions generated or the intuitive sensations can reveal a great deal of information.

✧ Continue to hold the crystal, moving it around within your hands. Clairvoyant pictures may follow automatically, but if not picture the blue dot expanding into a screen within your mind. Wait and one image will follow another.

✧ Clairaudient words or phrases may come into your mind, whether warnings or opportunities to be seized, or a message from a guide or your wise inner self. Though this is the most common order of psychic information, if you are experienced they will occur concurrently.

✧ If working with a client, ask them what they sense, hear and see and then hold the crystal yourself. Give your findings which you can then combine.

✧ I have deliberately not yet mentioned the individual crystal meanings in detail. Though I have given template meanings for the twelve crystals your psychic powers can identify their inherent properties to guide you to the right meaning. However, knowing the background of each additional crystal can help to fine-tune your readings, so read about the properties of any new crystal you add to your set.

✧ To choose extra crystals, go to a mineral store and hold your hands over different kinds and colours to guide you, or run your index finger a few centimetres away from online illustrations to select what you need. The more kinds you read with, the richer the information.

USING YOUR CRYSTALS IN YOUR CLAIRVOYANT WORK

✧ In order to answer a specific question about the future, pick three crystals, one at a time, from the bag without looking as you ask your question.

✧ Hold each crystal separately and then finally all three together.

✧ Once you have added at least another six different crystals to your basic set, you can, if you wish, choose and hold six crystals instead of three, first separately and then all together.

✧ Practise by asking friends, colleagues or family to pick a crystal from the bag without looking. If you are working professionally, add this on to any therapeutic practice.

✧ I would recommend picking a daily crystal in the morning and if it is a significant day, carry the crystal with you as a talisman in a tiny purse for the day to release its powers.

THE CRYSTALS

✧ The first time you use your set of twelve crystals, wash each one before you begin and set them in a circle round a lighted white candle. Do the same whenever you add new crystals to your set.

✧ Light a lemon, pine, juniper or thyme incense stick from the candle and spiral it over the crystal circle, saying three times, 'I ask that my crystals will be filled with light and speak only the truth with kindness.'

✧ Pass each crystal in turn over the candle flame.

✧ Leave the candle and incense burning while you work.

✧ Before and after any subsequent crystal session waft an incense stick over them or sprinkle them with water to cleanse them.

1) Clear quartz crystal

Powers it offers: The stone of the sun, pure life force, good health, wealth, happiness, energy and new beginnings; transforms negativity into positive light energies; clears stagnation; fathering issues. The stone of the life force.

Divinatory significance: Be optimistic about a planned new beginning or about the success of any venture. Anything is possible if you really want it and are prepared to go all out.

2) Purple amethyst

Powers it offers: Heals any ills; anti-stress stone; the reduction of addictions, fears and phobias and destructive love. Calms excess emotions, nightmares and mood swings; use amethyst to amplify spiritual and psychic powers and protect against unfriendly para-normal or negative earth energies.

Divinatory significance: Trust your intuition and listen to your dreams. Give yourself more private time: say no to others' unreasonable demands, cut down unnecessary work commitments and avoid critical people.

3) Green aventurine (alternative: jade)

Powers it offers: The ultimate good luck charm; stone of travel and travellers; protective against accidents of all kinds; helpful at work for solving problems and for generating original ideas.

Divinatory significance: An excellent time to take a chance even if it seems a risk; visit a place you have always wanted or plan some spontaneous fun or relaxation.

4) Orange carnelian (alternative: amber)

Powers it offers: The stone of courage and also of independent action, self confidence and creativity; for self-employment and freedom from restrictions; also fertility in every way.

Divinatory significance: Decide what would make you happy, even if others would not consider this fulfilment. Do not accept second best, believe in yourself and develop your creative talents, maybe into a viable venture.

5) Yellow citrine

Powers it offers: The happiness stone for individuals, families and the workplace; good for communication of all kinds and for employment matters; called the merchant's stone; ensures money flows into your home or business; assists healing through conventional medical treatment.

Divinatory significance: A good time for socialising, emailing, texting and telephoning, especially people far away or with whom you have lost touch; for success in tests, interviews or examinations. Beware, however, those who would deceive.

6) Red jasper (alternative: red tiger's eye)

Powers it offers: Strength; success through persistence; stamina; overcoming obstacles and inertia in self and others; passion; all physical activities.

Divinatory significance: Refuse to take no for an answer. Channel negative feelings into tackling injustice, bullying or prejudice assertively but in a controlled manner; make things happen rather than talking about them.

7) Pink rose quartz

Powers it offers: Self-love of yourself as you are and attracting lasting love and people you can trust; good for mending quarrels; for peace, happy families and healing the past; for alternative methods of healing.

Divinatory significance: Do not undervalue yourself or allow others to diminish your self-esteem. You may be called on to act as peacemaker and bring healing to a person, situation or relationship; children, the home and animals bring happiness.

8) Grey smoky quartz

Powers it offers: Protective in the home and when travelling, especially if alone; light at the end of your particular tunnel; patience; the keeping of secrets and the ability to adapt to the current situation. The stone of hope.

Divinatory significance: Improvement in a situation or relationship that may have drained you of hope and energy, especially worries about ill-health, family, career or debt; someone you have given up on may prove worthwhile after all.

9) Lapis lazuli (alternative: dark blue sodalite)

Powers it offers: Harmony, balance and the ability to speak wisely and if necessary compromise; for steady career advancement; helpful for any legal, business or official matters; good against fears of flying (sodalite); for older women.

Divinatory significance: Check facts and figures and consider both sides of the argument before making a decision; justice will be done through conventional channels; what you fear will not come to pass.

10) Brown tiger's eye

Powers it offers: Prosperity, financial gains, successful home and property ventures; stability materially and emotionally; good or improving health.

Divinatory significance: Good fortune in financial terms and for any DIY or buying/selling a home; vehicle or new possessions; a symbol of abundance and successful hospitality and family or home celebrations.

11) Black jet (alternative: obsidian)

Powers it offers: Protection against negative attitudes or emotional vampires, bad or noisy neighbours and the excesses of modern technology and machinery; preserves what is of value and old traditions.

Divinatory significance: The tried and trusted is better right now than excitement; mend rather than cast off, whether a relationship or venture; unexpected support will come your way, but avoid people who overload you with their sorrows.

12) Creamy shimmering moonstone (alternative: soft white selenite)

Powers it offers: Fertility, good relationships with mothers and all mothering issues; intuitive wisdom; connection with the natural cycles of personal energy flows and ebbs and those of nature; enhanced psychic powers.

Divinatory significance: Take steps towards fulfilling a discarded dream; follow your instincts about a person or offer, whatever the apparent external factors. Remember the easiest path is not always the right one.

CLAIRAUDIENCE AND CLAIRVOYANCE

The following exercise involves attuning to the sounds of other dimensions through your inner or psychic voice, which is linked with the blue Throat chakra sphere that also rules the ears.

WORKING WITH THE VOICES OF NATURE

The sound of the wind through the trees will transmit messages from wise forest essences or from Zuphlas, the angel of the forest, who is often asked to bless clairaudience from the trees.

Each species of tree has its own particular sound and focus of wisdom: the pine, inspiration and creativity; the ash, healing and travel; and the shimmering silver birch, new beginnings. Every land has its indigenous divinatory trees whose messages you can channel.

✧ Begin when it is windy.

✧ Ask the protection of Zuphlas, the angel of the forest, and the essences of the trees you are going to work with, whether you regard them as nature beings from another dimension or part of the essential life force.

✧ Before asking a question, listen to the rhythm of the wind and the blowing leaves and you will become attuned to the psychic voice manifest through the physical sounds that some people hear as a chorus of voices or as a single one. Generally tree wisdom is not immediately obvious but begins trains of thought that will offer keys to understanding a current relevant matter in your life.

✧ Experiment with different species of trees, a mixed grove or a large leafy individual tree and in different weather conditions. Trees like the white poplar or aspen traditionally shake with virtually no wind.

✧ When you are confident, go to your favourite trees when there is no wind or rain and listen. Be patient and you will in time hear the woodland voice within your mind, without the physical movement of the leaves, and then you know you are totally tuned into your clairaudient voice and ear.

✧ Before long you will spontaneously begin to hear messages in other voices of nature: the rain beating on the roof, the crashing of the sea or a fast flowing river.

CLAIRSENTIENCE AND CLAIRVOYANCE

Clairsentience, our psychic antennae or radar, is already finely tuned into both our own and the universal energy field and so rarely needs developing separately. Its closest psychic sense is psychometry: when you touch an artefact in an old building, what you feel or sense will be usually the first psychic information you receive. If you want to specifically practise clairsentience, you can work with timeless fragrances as described on pages 136–137.

PSYCHOMETRY AND CLAIRVOYANCE

Psychometry is a direct method of reading the aura or energy field that artefacts and places have accumulated round them. This energy field is built up from the thoughts, experiences and emotions of those who have handled the objects that are imprinted on the aether or spiritual energy plane. Sometimes experienced mediums will ask for a small treasure belonging to a deceased person in order to establish a clear line of contact with the bereaved. An object that belongs to a living individual and is frequently carried or used by them can also act as a transmitter for the energy field of the owner and reveal his or her unique blueprint of future possibilities.

PSYCHOMETRY OF A PLACE

This is the easiest form of psychometry for a beginner and as you practise you may as a result of touching the walls or furniture in an old building be able to see in your mind, or even three-dimensionally, the people who once lived there. This aspect of psychometry is described in Chapter Nine on ghosts so you can practise it in the field.

PSYCHOMETRY USING ARTEFACTS CONNECTED WITH THE PAST OF A FAMILY

If you first work with artefacts that have history connected to them, there is much more aura information to discover than with a relatively new item. Work with items or small pieces of furniture belonging to friends and acquaintances that have been in their family for generations and whose past is known in more detail, but not by you.

Before beginning, especially if you go on to work with items of unknown origin, perhaps at an antique fair or an industrial museum, splash the centre of your brow with water and ask the blessings of those who have owned the items over the years. Then hold your hands several centimetres above the item to find the outer limits of its aura. This will feel sticky, almost like a thin layer of rubber that is starting to melt. Artefacts only have a single aura layer that tends to be white, grey or silver. You may be able to see the aura in your mind's eye or externally. You will sense the energy field as waves of rippling energy. Your hands will tingle with the energy. If you feel a knotted or tangled area probe gently with your fingers for that may signify some major event or perhaps trauma to an owner or the place it was kept.

Then stroke the object until you feel the hard physical boundaries of the treasure softening and its energies flowing into your hands. Picture the first set of hands holding the object. As that contact fades, imagine another pair of hands being given the object to hold. In doing so you are clairvoyantly witnessing the item being handed down from generation to generation. Alternatively, you can work backwards from the present owner. If the owner is present, keep talking without checking with them, as this would break the psychic flow. Be open to the unexpected and at first do not expect to pick up more than one or two emotions or events. If you are working alone keep a Dictaphone running and speak aloud. You may also pick up current issues, especially if there is a family crisis, strong emotion or the item is still used regularly.

ANSWERING QUESTIONS

✧ Establish what the questioner needs to know about the future as precisely as possible.

✧ Ask the questioner to let you hold the object. The object is acting as a channel since it is imprinted with the questioner's aura and so holds information about the potential future of the person.

✧ Begin as in the previous exercise by feeling the energy around the item and then holding it.

✧ Some clairvoyants do see clear scenes of the object in the questioner's life, but generally the information is all about the person. Again, keep talking and then afterwards you can make sense of information you received with the questioner. If you stop to check if you are right, you block your intuitions and switch to analytical questioning. You may then find yourself guessing or deducing rather than using psychic power.

✧ In psychometry the messages may be partly in symbols that have meaning to the recipient rather than the clairvoyant, so ask about any symbols that seem especially vivid.

PSYCHOKINESIS AND CLAIRVOYANCE

PENDULUM POWER

A pendulum, most commonly a pointed clear quartz crystal on a chain, provides an external demonstration of psychokinesis, as the hand automatically moves the direction of the pendulum in response to the promptings of the unconscious mind. In some cases it is believed the direction is influenced by an angel or guide. The pendulum movement can identify a correct decision or locate a missing object, person or animal, paranormal presences or subterranean energies whether psychic energy lines or leys, water, oil or minerals. The pendulum amplifies the clairvoyant's own inner radar. At the end of the chapter we will practise inner dowsing without the pendulum (see page 86.)

How Should You Hold a Pendulum?

Hold the chain between the thumb and forefinger of the hand you write with, though do experiment with the other hand. There are no definitive rights or wrongs. Wind any extra chain around the index finger of the same hand. Recommended chain lengths vary from about 23cm to as long as feels comfortable so the pendulum becomes an extension of your arm. For outdoor dowsing, earth energy or ghost work indoors, about 38cm is ideal. But some people like a really short chain.

Establishing the Pendulum's Responses

If you are new to pendulum work, you need to establish your pendulum's yes/no response.

An easy way is to deliberately move the pendulum in circles clock-wise and ask the pendulum to always indicate a positive response with the movement you are making. You can then select an appropriate negative response, for example an anticlockwise movement, and ask the pendulum to always use that.

However, if you prefer you can use the following method to discover the pendulum's own natural movements:

✧ Gently set your pendulum in motion.

✧ To find your personal yes response, visualise a very happy or successful moment in your life.

✧ The pendulum will respond to the recalled positive emotion with its yes response, usually a clockwise circle or ellipse.

✧ To discover your personal pendulum's no response, concentrate on a time when you felt disappointed. A no pendulum movement is generally the opposite mirror image of the yes response.

Decision-making with Pendulums

✧ Write down your initial question or say it out loud.

✧ Let your mind go blank by visualising a night sky with the stars going out one by one, leaving inky blackness.

✧ If you hold the pendulum in a static position it will begin to move. The stronger the circling motion or speed, the more definite the yes or no answer is.

✧ Ask another question if you wish, allowing this to emerge spontaneously. Continue until you have no more questions.

✧ Remember the question must be formulated to elicit a yes or no in response. If you want to know a time frame to the question, ask the pendulum to indicate, by the number of positive swings it makes, the number of days, weeks, months or even years before the desired event.

Dowsing for Options

There is a second method of pendulum dowsing that can be used to decide between a number of options.

◇ Choose an issue in which you have several choices and ask the pendulum to indicate by vibrating and/or pulling downwards the correct decision.

◇ Divide a piece of A4 paper into squares and write as many options as you have in different squares. It does not matter if some are blank. You can also draw a chart of numbers to dowse for your lucky lottery numbers.

◇ If moving home, use pictures of houses for sale to decide which would be best for you. You can do the same with hotels when going on holiday.

◇ Set small pots of herbs, essential oils or different remedies from your medicine chest in a circle to dowse for the best to ease a particular condition.

◇ Test different foods and drinks to discover which your body needs right now or which cause allergies. If you cannot dowse over the actual objects substitute them with written names.

Method:

◇ Hold your pendulum in turn over each of the marked options or items, moving it very slowly from left to right and top to bottom on a chart of options.

◇ The sensation you are seeking is a strong pull of the pendulum downwards over one of the named options. The pendulum may become very heavy prior to pulling down.

◇ Unless you feel an instant pull over one square or object pass the pendulum over the whole grid or items.

✧ Continue even if you have made a choice. You may notice a less intense tugging over one or even two other squares. These can indicate additional useful factors or options.

I have written extensively about finding what is lost with a pendulum using signals from the aura of the person, object or animal that is missing (see Chapter Ten).

PSYCHOKINESIS AND AUTOMATIC WRITING

Automatic writing is another psychokinetic power whereby the hand will write information that is not consciously realised. The wisdom enters via the four outermost of the seven layers of your aura, or personal energy field, and filters into your Heart chakra – linked with the fourth layer of the aura. This chakra controls the hands and arms – and so the pen.

Automatic writing is also a powerful method of decision-making and of creative inspiration for would-be authors, poets, playwrights, songwriters and for brainstorming for ideas at work or creatively.

PREPARING FOR AUTOMATIC WRITING

✧ You will need pen and paper: traditionally green ink and cream paper.

✧ Touch the centre of your hairline with a single drop of water, picture white, gold and violet light pouring in and say, 'Above me is light.' You may feel a tingling sensation.

✧ Next anoint the centre of your brow with another drop of water, seeing lilac and indigo light entering and say 'Within me is radiance.' You may feel sudden warmth.

✧ As you next anoint the centre of your throat, visualise sky blue light entering and say, 'That I may write wisely.'

✧ Finally anoint each wrist pulse point and imagine rich green light pouring into your body, saying 'The love in my heart.' You may feel peace flowing right through your body. You may now feel the hand you write with tingling.

✧ Light a white candle.

✧ Write your first question at the top of the paper and read it aloud slowly. Hold the pen in a relaxed way in the hand you normally write with and allow the words to flow through your pen on to the paper without trying to rationalise or analyse.

✧ When the pen slows, before reading, write another question if you wish. You can ask a series of questions.

✧ When you sense there is no more to come, put down the pen.

✧ Gently touch your wrist points, first the right and then the left, with the index finger of your power hand to close your Heart chakra. Close your other three higher chakras in the same way.

✧ If you sense the information is coming from an angel or guide, you can thank them before closing the chakras.

✧ Read the information by candlelight, adding more candles if it is after dark. Then blow out the candle/s and say, 'May all be as it was before. Blessings be on all.'

FOLLOW-UP ACTIVITIES AND RESEARCH

✧ To improve your psychokinetic powers try dowsing without a pendulum to draw you to what you need.

✧ Picture the energy field round a desired place, situation, person or object not yet in your life as a clear white light. Imagine as many details as you can of the chosen item or situation. Extend both arms so you make an arch round your head and shoulders. Feel the soft rubbery membrane of the outermost layer of your aura and picture yourself surrounded by a rainbow. The coloured bands become more clearly defined the closer they move to the body and enclose you in a rainbow sphere.

✧ Imagine a line of white light, a series of small lights, the psi or psychic line of connection, extending from your brow to the desired object, person or situation.

✧ Now picture yourself as you follow the psi line in your mind and later maybe in actuality towards what you are visualising. If in doubt hold your hands palms outwards vertically to tune into the energies of what you desire. You may instantly know where to go to find what you seek and the means to get there or obtain what you want. At the same time a person or opportunity may be called psychokinetically towards you.

SIX

Learning and Perfecting Basic Clairvoyant Systems

In previous chapters you learned about the crystal ball, geomancy and divination with small crystals. In this chapter I discuss tarot, runes and tree staves. There are many other systems apart from the three I am focusing on here, such as palmistry, astrology and numerology. These can be learned from books and online.

TAROT

Whether you are a beginner or a tarot expert, spend time focusing on the pictures of the pack and pick a card every day (see page 23 for suggestions of packs).

✧ Hold the card and, breathing gently and slowly, imagine the card as a world which you can enter.

✧ Note anything of significance in the picture and if you wish check the conventional meaning if you do not know it. If a card appears regularly you know that it has a particular message for you. When you are more experienced, work with more than one pack in more general readings as if a card appears twice you know it is of significance.

✧ When you read for clients, ask what they see in each picture and what they feel as they look at it.

✧ Ignore reversals – upside down cards – as usually these have just been put back that way during the previous session. No card is inherently bad or unlucky and the reading will determine whether a challenging or positive aspect is most in evidence.

✧ Unless you have a favourite spread or layout, try building up an open reading with nine cards as three horizontal rows of three, selected from a shuffled pack. Then add a crowning tenth card if you wish. A spread that pre-assigns positions can limit you unfolding the full significance of each card and of creatively combining different related cards within the reading.

✧ If any card appears unhelpful to the questioner or refers to a past issue best forgotten, remove it from the spread and ask the questioner to pick a substitute card from the pack. For choosing between options, select a single card to represent the question and then beneath it create a vertical descending row for each of the options you have. Each row could have two, three or four cards and you can lay a row at a time or one for each row and then the second for each row.

The following are template meanings for people who are unfamiliar with tarot. Remember, the essence of tarot is always the relationship between the questioner, the picture on the card, the issue under question and the interpreter. The pack is either numbered 0–21(Fool through to the World) or 1–22 according to the creator of the set. If you are interested in the numerological significance of the number order I have written a detailed chapter in *Cassandra Eason's Complete Book of Tarot*. This topic is quite complicated but may be of interest to more experienced practitioners.

THE MAJOR ARCANA

0 The Fool: Take a chance, go for the unexpected choice or sudden opportunity; follow your instincts and reclaim your essential spontaneity and joy in life.

Challenges: A too good to be true offer may be just that, so do not leave your common sense behind.

1 The Magician: Be creative, use your initiative, put your plans into action for the time is right; be versatile, especially in business affairs, and approach existing problems from a new angle. A new charismatic exciting person may enter your life.

Challenges: Beware of committing yourself too fast as the Magician can be a con artist or fantasist.

2 The High Priestess or Popess: Make time for yourself and develop your emerging spiritual side; keep your own and other people's secrets, seek personal fulfilment rather than success in other people's eyes.

Challenges: Avoid seeking perfection at all costs or becoming disillusioned if people make mistakes.

3 The Empress: Be generous with your time and encourage those who need your support; fertility and abundance will enter your life in the way most needed; mothering/nurturing is a major and positive feature of the days ahead.

Challenges: Avoid giving too much to others and discourage overdependency on you or feeling guilty.

4 The Emperor: Acknowledge or claim your power, aim high and go for whatever it is you want; be prepared to take the lead and to stick to your principles; fathering or authority issues or a powerful man in your life.

Challenges: Resist pressure or bullying from a strongly critical older person or authority figure, usually male.

5 The Hierophant or Pope: Be cautious and avoid the seemingly easy path or short cut; follow the conventional or traditional route in learning, training or acquiring wisdom and develop your spiritual learning path; a wise teacher or counsellor will become significant.

Challenges: Do not listen to voices in your head from the past, whether critical people or memory of earlier past failure.

6 The Lovers: Choices in love and maybe a new lover, the growth of existing love or the rekindling of a love grown cold or indifferent, can indicate the presence or arrival of a twin soul.

Challenges: If you follow a deep love with someone not free, or a lover who will not commit, there will be a cost that you need to weigh up.

7 The Chariot: Take control of the direction of your life and make the changes *you* want; travel opportunities or the need for a holiday or short break; disruption may open doors.

Challenges: Avoid changing or leaving a situation or the people around you if the problem is your own inner restlessness.

8 Strength, Force or Fortitude: If you persist then you can overcome any obstacles or opposition, no matter how daunting; use persuasion to get what you want; a long-standing problem will soon be resolved if you are patient; increasing health and energy.

Challenges: Do not continue to pour effort into a lost cause or relationship.

9 The Hermit: Withdraw from situations where you are always the peacemaker; wait rather than act; listen to your inner voice and follow your own path, even if it is not that of others; your inner psychic powers are emerging naturally; a kind older person of either sex with experience and compassion.

Challenges: Beware inertia, self-induced isolation or relying too much on experts.

10 The Wheel of Fortune: Good fortune or opportunity is returning to your life or, if things are going well, will continue; choices and actions now will have beneficial effects in the future; good for speculation, especially in money matters.

Challenges: Believing that the future is fixed and so accepting a down turn rather than trying to turn the wheel upwards yourself.

11 Justice: Any legal or official matters will turn out well; a time to act or speak out against injustice – but also to let go what cannot be resolved.

Challenges: Feeling you have no right to fair treatment in any aspect of life and settling for second best.

12 The Hanged Man: Give up what is holding you back; what you do now will bear fruit in the future, even if it involves short-term sacrifices or loss.

Challenges: Do not sacrifice yourself for an unworthy cause or give an unreliable or unworthy person too many chances.

13 Death: Close the door on a situation or relationship that no longer makes you happy or is going nowhere; the necessary natural progression from one stage of life to another that may cause regrets.

Challenges: Fear of loss or betrayal that may actually precipitate it through possessiveness or jealousy.

14 Temperance: Hope and light at the end of the tunnel for you; avoid excesses of all kinds; personal harmony and inner balance; the restoration of health; the way forward is through compromise and peacemaking.

Challenges: Avoid keeping the peace between continually warring factions at the expense of your inner harmony.

15 The Devil: Express negative feelings.

Challenges: Avoid giving way to temptation that may hurt you or others.

16 The Tower (of liberation): Break out of old restrictions imposed by others or your own past actions even if it causes disruption; learn from the mistakes of the past; changes you may have resisted will bring freedom; see what can be salvaged from what did not work out.

Challenges: Avoid repeating the same mistakes.

17 The Star: You can make your dreams come true whatever your age or stage of life, so do not be sidetracked; a good time to develop or revive creative, media, performing, craft or artistic talents; recognition in the way most needed, even occasionally fame.

Challenges: Spending all your life dreaming and not trying.

18 The Moon: Allow your emotions, not logic, to guide you; trust your intuition; a good sign for psychic and spiritual development, fertility matters, babies, children, young girls, imaginative projects and for going with the flow of life.

Challenges: Live more in the real world if you are to make things happen.

19 The Sun: The best card in the pack, promising happiness, and success in the world's terms, the chance to develop your potential. Enjoy every moment of happiness; good for sporting and leisure activities.

Challenges: Excess sun burns; avoid overwork and losing sight of what you are working for.

20 Judgement/Rebirth: Today is the day you worried about yesterday and represents a chance for a new beginning; don't judge yourself too harshly or accept unfair criticism from others.

Challenges: Blaming others or circumstances and not accepting you made mistakes too.

21 The World: Anything is possible; advantageous travel, house and career moves, expanding business interests, especially via the

Internet, an unexpected gift or offer. Start walking towards where you want to go and who you want to go with and Lady Luck will follow.

Challenges: Make sure it is *your* dream you are moving towards, not just to please someone you love.

THE MINOR ARCANA

Combine the suit meanings and the number meanings below to understand the significance of the Minor Cards.

Pentacles, Discs or Coins (Earth): Material security, stability, the practical organisation of our daily lives, home, family, animals, financial matters, property – especially homes and house moves; dealings with officialdom and financial institutions.

Challenges: Meanness, over-caution, materialism, over-emphasis on the past and what is familiar.

Cups or Chalices (Water): Love, friendship, fidelity, psychic powers and the environment; love affairs as yet undiscovered, long-standing partnerships and marriage, personal harmony, fertility, alternative healing, beauty and reconciliation.

Challenges: Sentimentality, indecisiveness, manipulation, possessiveness.

Wands, Rods or Staves (Fire): Creativity, originality, independence, courage, individuality, untapped possibilities, creative and artistic ventures, male potency, travel, spontaneous house moves or relocations, health, self-confidence and self-esteem.

Challenges: Impulsivity, irritability, fickleness, unreliability.

Swords (Air): Logic, focus, rational thought, courage, career matters, action and change, determination, clear communication, speculation, all matters scientific and technological and conventional medicine, therapy and surgery, justice, learning and the law, also overcoming challenges and obstacles.

Challenges: Carelessness with others' feelings, selfishness and lack of loyalty, crippling fears.

Aces: New beginnings, new opportunities, new people or restored energies, good luck and health coming into your life.

The Twos: Balance and compromise, harmony between two people or life paths, the ability or need to do more than one thing at once; also the need to make a choice between two people, demands or opportunities.

The Threes: Building or rebuilding of existing situations or decisions; traditionally associated with pregnancy and birth, the gradual success of all creative ventures.

The Fours: Caution or taking a risk is the question and dilemma of the fours; a desire for more in life than the everyday world offers versus stability and security.

The Fives: Winning through in spite of obstacles and opposition; facing situations as they are and deciding if you want to carry on, look further afield or quit.

The Sixes: Harmony in your life, with others and within yourself; coming back to your roots and what matters most; restoring the balance between what you give and what you get back.

The Sevens: Contemplation, assessing and reaping what has been gained and what has been lost; distinguishing false friends from true and defending your principles and rights.

The Eights: Speculation about or embracing of new opportunities; the loss of fear or illusion; abandoning the redundant; learning new skills; self-employment or a second career using your talents sometimes later in life.

The Nines: Self-confidence, self-esteem, independence, desire for perfection; personal achievement and happiness rather than through others, the need for a final effort to achieve a dream.

The Tens: Perfection, achievement of goals, the end of a struggle; lasting joy and security with others; the need to preserve what is of worth and lasting, and close doors on what is not.

THE COURT CARDS

Combine the rank of the personality with the suit meanings as they relate to personalities.

The Pages: The Pages refer to a girl or a sensitive boy, a younger teenager of either sex or a woman of any age who is not in a committed relationship or values freedom over putting down roots. The card can also represent an undeveloped aspect of the questioner's personality or talents or the first tentative steps towards a new life phase.

The Knights: Knights are usually young boys or older teenagers of either sex. They can also represent young men or men of any age who are still uncommitted or, if they are, retain their desire for freedom. The card can also represent our enthusiasm and a burst of energy for a venture or relationship or a positive change.

The Queens: Queens represent older women, whether in age or maturity. They can also be a female authority or mothering figure. The card also signifies that you are entering a fertile and creative or caring (not just in the sense of babies) period of your life (whether you are male or female).

The Kings: Kings represent mature or older men. They often represent mentors or authority figures in your life or financial, official and legal institutions. Kings symbolise power and success or the determination to achieve a particular goal, in either sex.

RUNES

Runes are angular markings on stone, wood or crystal, each of which relates to a human issue or quality. You can buy ready-made runes. Alternatively make your own by drawing in red permanent pen or painting in red the symbols below on twenty-four round or oval stones the size of a medium coin. Keep them in a red drawstring bag.

✧ The first time you use your runes, set them in a circle around a lit red candle. Sprinkle three circles of salt around them and then circle a lighted sage smudge or pine incense stick to create three more circles of smoke and say, 'By Odin, Thor, Frigg and Freya be blessed.' Thor was the protective thunder god, Odin the Father God who is credited with discovering the runes, Frigg the mother goddess and mistress of prophecy, and Freya the goddess of beauty who taught magic to the deities. Leave the candle and smudge to burn through.

✧ Pick three marked runes from your twenty-four in the bag without looking and cast them either on a square white cloth about two metres wide or within a circle of similar size drawn in earth or sand. Indoors, light a red candle and cast the runes on your table or within a circle drawn in a tray or earth or sand, about a metre in circumference.

✧ Read any runes that fall marked side up and continue throwing lots of three till you have at least three uppermost and have answered your question. If necessary, return the blank-sided ones you have cast to the bag. Hold each rune as you read it and allow feelings, words and impressions to supplement the meanings.

THE RUNE AETTS OR SETS

As you read the meanings you will make obvious links between the symbols of the runes and tarot. Note any correlations and how often they occur in readings. The first aett or set of eight runes is dedicated to Freya.

Fehu, Cattle/wealth

Cattle were the tangible sign of wealth and could, if necessary, be transported to a new land.

Divinatory meanings: Prosperity, security, successful property negotiations, the reduction of financial problems, unexpected luck, the price that must be paid for change or happiness.

Uruz, Wild cattle, primal strength

The horns of these huge untamable fierce oxen were worn on Viking helmets to transfer the strength of the creature to warriors.

Divinatory meanings: Successful business risks and speculation, improving health, a huge effort to overcome obstacles, strength and courage.

Thurisaz, the hammer of Thor

Thor's hammer defended the deities against the frost giants and was a sacred symbol at marriages, births and funerals.

Divinatory meanings: The need for protection, overcoming challenges and conflicts, male potency, passion, fertility and secrets.

Ansuz, the Mouth, Odin, the God

The name for Odin, God of poetry and communication, who hung from the World Tree for nine days and nine nights to obtain the wisdom of the runes.

Divinatory meanings: Continuing or reviving good luck, passing tests and examinations or interviews, for all literary and artistic ventures, the need for clear communication and a chance to take the lead/promotion.

Raidho, the Wheel, the Wagon, Riding

The long and dangerous but exciting ride and also the sun moving through the year.

Divinatory meanings: Travel and career opportunities or relocation, success in legal matters and the need to seize opportunity even in less than ideal circumstances.

Cenaz or Kenaz, the torch, illumination

The Cosmic Fire that fused with ice and brought about the creation of the Norse universe. It is also the pine resin torch that illuminated great halls and humble homesteads alike in the darkest winter.
Divinatory meanings: Trust intuition and the inner voice, sudden illumination and the solution of a problem, the fulfilment of anything that is intensely desired, consummation of love, conception of a child.

Gebo, the Gift or giving

The marriage and committed relationship rune and sharing good fortune and also of evolving psychic gifts.
Divinatory meanings: Ask for what you need from others as you may be giving too much; joy in relationships, especially concerning fidelity or commitment issues; an unexpected bonus.

Wunjo, Joy

The light on the growing fields, indicating the blessings of the deities.

Divinatory meanings: Ask what would make you happy and fulfilled rather than focusing on the happiness and well-being of others; a good time to ask for promotion or advancement, for self-employment and to release the hold anyone has over you.

The second aett is dedicated to Heimdall, the Watcher God and Guardian of the Rainbow Bridge that spanned the dimension between Asgard, the realm of the gods, and Midgard, the world of mortals.

Hagalaz, Hail

The rune of the cosmic seed, the ice that met the fire in creation, the frozen seed within that melts to bring life-giving water.

Divinatory meanings: Embrace necessary change or disruption by natural events and within a few months transformation and rewards will result; a good time to quit a bad habit or overcome a fear or phobia.

Naudhiz, the Need or Ritual fire

The wooden spindle that generates the festival fire by friction, to release, it was believed, the fire within the wood.

Divinatory meanings: If your needs are not being met say so; alternatively you have within yourself all the necessary gifts to succeed and to be self-reliant; the kindling of passion and also for attracting love in a difficult situation.

Isa, Ice

The rune of Ice, the fifth element in the Norse tradition and associated with an ice bridge between dimensions that needs to be negotiated with care, but must be crossed before the ice melts.

Divinatory meanings: A good time to begin any negotiations, reconciliation attempts, especially in love or with estranged family, and taking the first steps towards future change; wait for the right moment to act.

Jera, the Harvest

The good harvest blessed by the god of the earth Frey or Ing, consort of Nerthus or Berkano the earth goddess, depending on how well the seeds were sown in the spring and cared for.

Divinatory meanings: The results of earlier efforts will soon be realised, learn from old mistakes, the acquisition of material resources, success in legal matters, fertility and good fortune.

Eihwaz, the Yew tree

The longest living of trees and as an evergreen symbol at the Mid-Winter Solstice (the old Christmas) that spring would return; also the bow made from the yew wood.

Divinatory meanings: Use what you have and learn to make life more as you want it; the need to close doors and move on to new beginnings, value what is worth preserving in life and love.

Perthro, the Gambling cup and essential self

Gambling and divination were very close in function to the Vikings, and decisions would be made from casting runes to indicate the will of the deities.

Divinatory meanings: You will discover a secret or unknown information; value your real essential self rather than trying to fit into expectations; take a chance as it is a lucky time.

Elhaz or Algiz, Elk sedge, Elk or Eel grass

Lots of alternative meanings, a two-edged sword or sharp marsh grass that is useful but painful to hold; Elk sedge is an old expression for a two-edged sword; also the antlers of the elk and from this the higher evolved spiritual self.

Divinatory meanings: Seize opportunities or make a decision even if difficult or painful as this will clear the way for a very good future whether freedom from limitations or a new life path; spiritual work is favoured; bad luck will soon change; good for resolving employment problems.

Sowilo, the Sun

Another fire rune of power of the sun to destroy the winter ice, make crops grow and guide seafarers; in the world of the North where the sun was so precious.

Divinatory meanings: The most auspicious of runes for any aspect of life, especially health, happiness and career. Go for what you want and develop hidden talents.

The third Aett belongs to Tiu or Tiw, the God of Justice and of the guiding Pole Star.

Tiwaz, the Pole star, a guiding star

Tiw, the god of war and justice, after whom the star was called in the Norse world, sacrificed his sword hand to bind Fenris Wolf to protect his father Odin.

Divinatory meanings: Favourable for all public performances, competitions and success in the performing arts or fame; also the need to pursue personal dreams and decide your own future; good for matters of justice and recovery from illness.

Berkano, the Birch tree, the Mother Goddess

Berkano is another name for the old Nordic earth mother Nerthus and the sowing of the crops; also of the birch tree that has the ability to reproduce itself.

Divinatory meanings: A time for new beginnings and revival of what was thought lost; good for mothering in all aspects and for starting up business initiatives or new creative projects based on innate skills to bear fruit six months further on.

Ehwaz, the Horse

A sacred animal to the Vikings, especially the horse that carried its rider into battle and so a symbol of perfect trust and harmony with another person or within the self.

Divinatory meanings: Indicates a swift resolution of a matter or the need for a fast response, travel, holiday, house moves and relocation, good for business partnerships and the restoration of harmony in a relationship or family and the resolution of power struggles or bullying.

Mannaz, Man, humankind

The first man and woman were formed by Odin and his brothers Vili and Ve from an ash and an elm and it was their descendants who would repopulate the new world after the destruction of the old.

Divinatory meanings: Do not expect to be Superman or -woman and ask for help and support if necessary; equally someone close may have acted thoughtlessly but the situation can be salvaged; a new skill will become easier.

Laguz, Water, the lake, the sea

The oak steeds, the name given to the Viking ships, launched on huge seas and some reached far-off lands against seemingly impossible odds. **Divinatory meanings:** If you want something enough you may have to face risks of failure or rejection; allow your emotions to guide you and flow with life rather than trying to swim against the prevailing trends.

Ingwaz, Fertility, the Fertility God

Ing or Frey drove his wagon over the fields after the winter to release the creative potential of the soil. He was also protective god of the hearth. **Divinatory meanings:** Launch a venture or initiate communication then wait for a response before going further or trying again; stop resources draining away; spend time with home and family or close friends; a good rune if you want a baby.

Othala, the homestead

Though the Norse people were great wanderers, the homestead was important to them and establishing the new homestead, with the blessings of the land guardians in the new land, was a priority.

Divinatory meanings: Blessings on the home, family pets and family finances; good for all house renovation projects, for successful re-location, improvements among older family members and possible family additions, for example, through marriage.

Dagaz, Day

Dagaz refers to the radiant youth Daeg, who opened the gates of each new day and brought back the light.

Divinatory meanings: Light at the end of the tunnel; life will get better; new skills, training opportunities or a second career, often later in life; a better situation concerning a young person.

CELTIC TREE OR OGHAM STAVES

This system is based on the Celtic system of angular ogham symbols, dedicated to the God Ogma. It is based on the significance of different trees. There are similarities with rune meanings (for example

Beith and *Berkano* both mean the birch tree and mother/maiden).

You can cast tree staves immediately after runes. Tree staves also combine well with crystal divination and home-made angel or goddess cards (see pages 73–77 and page 119).

WORKING WITH TREE STAVES

You can buy tree staves. Better still, create your own using twenty-one twigs of the same size, each about 13–16 centimetres long.

✧ Scrape the bark off the front of one side and paint or carve the symbol, marking with a line under it to indicate the bottom of the stave (as some signs are similar).

✧ Leave the twenty-first stave blank.

✧ Keep them in a pouch or bag of any natural substance.

✧ Cast tree staves as for runes on to the ground or a table, using the same cloth or surface, but in twos not threes.

✧ Read the staves that fall uppermost, continuing till you have a minimum of two symbols uppermost.

✧ Visualise and find out more about the myths of the different trees and also their special creatures and crystals and these will add to the deeper significance of the meaning.

✧ Where possible look for the actual trees, or if they do not grow in your area, substitute indigenous trees with similar properties or myths.

THE MEANINGS OF THE TREE STAVES

Beith: Birch (Betula pendula)

Tree of the Mother Goddess, birch trees were planted in front of dwellings to invoke the protection of the Earth Mother. The birch is symbolic also of the Spring Maiden's birth.

In divination: New beginnings and regeneration, fresh opportunities or perspectives, self-employment or personal initiative.
Special creature: White stag
Crystal: Clear quartz

Luis: Rowan or Mountain Ash (Sorbus aucuparia)

Rowan traditionally protects households, people and animals against bewitchment and harmful ghosts and natural disasters; also used in dowsing to find minerals.

In divination: Launch creative ventures, and find new opportunities; protect yourself and loved ones against malice and conflict; a time for unexpected guests, psychic powers grow.
Special creature: Dragon
Crystal: Selenite

Fearn: Alder (Alnus glutinosa)

The Alder is the tree of fire, known as the tree of Bran, the Celtic warrior God who gave his life for the land. Because of its resistance to water, alder was used for piles on which early houses were built over lakes or marshy land.

In divination: Follow a slow path in building and rebuilding and ventures will flourish; short-term sacrifice may be necessary; resist pressure to divert you from the right path.

Special creature: Raven/fox

Crystal: Red tiger's eye

Saille: Willow (Salix alba)

The Willow is sacred to Brighid, the Celtic triple Goddess of fire, inspiration, smiths, poets and healers, and at the beginning of February the maiden Brighid with her willow wand melted the snows of winter.

In divination: Good for love, for joy after sorrow and caring for others and also slowly melting coldness, opposition or anger. Trust your intuition, but beware illusions and secrecy by others.

Special creature: Hare

Crystal: Moonstone

Nuinn: Ash (Fraxinus excelsior)

The ash represents the World Tree that formed the axis of the universe and protected travellers overseas; the tree of healers.

In divination: The acquisition of resources, new friends and contacts; expand your horizons whether in travel, career advances

or in cyberspace; increasing healing powers.
Special creature: Kestrel or falcon
Crystal: Carnelian

Huathe: Hawthorn/whitethorn (Crataegus Oxyacantha)

The hawthorn heralded the Celtic summer on May morn when
the May blossoms were brought into houses to attract fertility.
In divination: Unexpected good luck, fertility in the way most
needed, creativity; the need to say no to unreasonable demands or
intrusions; closed doors may open.
Special creature: White horse
Crystal: Lapis lazuli

Duir: Oak (Quercus robur)

The oak is associated with the Celtic priesthood, the Druids who
traditionally studied for nineteen years, and the acorn likewise represents long-acquired wisdom from small beginnings as it takes many
years for a tree to evolve.
In divination: Opportunities for study or training, success of long-
term aims and goals; value what is long lasting over the superficial
and instant.
Special creature: Bear
Crystal: Amber

Tinne: Holly (Ilex aquifolium)

Holly was sacred to the Celtic God Taranis, the Thunder God/Giant and old Father Time.

In divination: Celebrations, cooperation from others; a reminder there is a time for everything and we need to accept and work within the constraints of life.

Special creature: Blackbird

Crystal: Red jasper

Coll: Hazel (Corylus avellana)

The Hazel is the Celtic tree of wisdom and the nine poetic nuts of inspiration hanging over the well of wisdom that stands in the Land of Eternal Youth.

In divination: Justice will be achieved by conventional means; seek expert opinion or improve your own expertise and if necessary compromise; good for writers or artists of any kind.

Special creature: Salmon

Crystal: Jade

Quert: Apple (Malus sylvestris)

This Tree of Life and of the sacred Isle of Avalon, whose fruit gave healing, rebirth and immortality to deities, heroes and humans alike, including King Arthur.

In divination: Love, good or improving health and energy, reconciliation in love, beauty, radiance, joy through babies, children and families.

Special creature: Hen

Crystal: Rose quartz

Muin: Vine (Vitis vinifera)/blackberry (Rubus fruticosus)

The vine was imported into Britain during the Bronze Age, though the native bramble or blackberry was used more frequently for wine-making.

In divination: Joy, seize the moment, seek what would make you happy and embrace new experiences; however, beware excesses of any kind.

Special creature: Swallow

Crystal: Amethyst

Gort: Ivy (Hedera helix)

Ivy was traditionally disliked since it choked the trees around which it grew. Yet it symbolised equally the loving and faithful Queen of winter, wife of the Holly King.

Divination: Fidelity and lasting commitment in love and loyalty in friends; beware however possessiveness and emotional manipulation.

Bird: Swan

Crystal: Moss agate (slow but steady growth in any area of life).

Ngetal: Wheat straw, reeds (Triticum/Phragmites)

In Ireland, in Celtic times a house was not established until the reed roof was in place to ensure the prosperity and the blessings of the deities. Wheat straw is symbol of the harvest.

In divination: Abundance in the way most needed; rewards for previous efforts made; the need to complete tasks or matters unfinished before moving on.

Special creature: Otter

Crystal: Aventurine

Straif: Blackthorn (Prunus spinosa)

The blackthorn is associated with Callieach, the Celtic Crone Goddess who cared for the herds in the coldest of winter; blackthorn blossoms early when it is still cold.

In divination: Effort and persistence will pay off even if the odds seem against you; a good omen for all matters concerning old worries and chronic illnesses; stay united with loved ones and fight your corner.

Special creature: Wolf

Crystal: Jet

Ruis: Elder (Sambucus nigra)

The Elder is the ultimate fairy tree and the tree of the midwife goddess who delivers the maiden of spring.

In divination: Trust your dreams and intuition; luck is all around you. You may decide to follow a different path or approach; information or services should be exchanged and help accepted.

Special creature: Badger

Crystal: Amethyst (substitute Purple flurorite)

Ailim: Pine/Silver Fir (Pinaceae/Abies alba)

The Pine was revered by the Celts as the pine resin torch could give light, ignite the forge, the fire of the hearth and ritual fires at sun festivals.

In divination: The way forward or answer becomes suddenly clear; remove what is no longer helpful in your life; make time and space for yourself.

Special creature: Phoenix (reborn every five hundred years)

Crystal: Obsidian

Onn: Bracken/Gorse (Pteridium aquilinum/Ulex europaeus)

Onn is sacred to the bee and honey goddess Ana, the Welsh Mother Goddess, and also the spring Gallic Goddess Onniona, when the gorse first blooms.

In divination: Sort out your paperwork, finances and life path; look for undeveloped talents as sources of income/happiness; a new learning process will become easier.

Animal: Bee
Crystal: Tiger's eye

Ur: Heather (Calluna vulgaris)

The Gallic Heather goddess was called Uroica, portrayed also as Queen Bee. The heather bloomed scarlet at midsummer and so came to be associated with passion and the sun.

In divination: Follow your heart whether in love or life as this is the time; happiness and good fortune; beware mistaking passion for love; explore undeveloped gifts and opportunities.

Special creature: Butterfly
Crystal: Rutilated quartz

Eadha: White Poplar (Populus alba)

The White Poplar tree of the Autumn Equinox, the late harvest, maturity and old age, is known as the shiver-tree because its leaves shook even with no breeze.

In divination: Forgive yourself for past mistakes and let go what cannot be put right or altered; you may need to act as peacemaker; your healing powers will increase; do not worry about older people.

Animal: Dove
Crystal: Sodalite

Ido/Ioho: Yew (Taxus baccata)

Breton myths tell that the yew extends a root into the mouth of each body in a graveyard, breathing new life into them; also a tree of long life and lasting love, living for two or three thousand years.

In divination: A good sign for lasting love, career, business and long life; what went wrong in your life can be rebuilt if you do not repeat mistakes; take life and decisions slowly.

Special creature: Eagle chick

Crystal: Fossils that contain the wisdom of the past

Mistletoe (Viscum album)

The blank tree stave. Called by the Druids the all healer and plucked from the oak tree at midwinter with a golden sickle. The mistletoe was never referred to by name as it was too sacred. It wasn't given a crystal or creature for the same reason.

In divination: Anything is possible; the small miracle, the dream or person you had given up on comes right.

INCORPORATING OTHER COMMERCIAL DIVINATORY SETS SUCH AS ANGELS, ANIMAL CARDS AND GODDESSES INTO CLAIRVOYANT SESSIONS

There are numerous sets of cards on the market and you may discover one that you can adopt to supplement existing clairvoyant methods. I often add three cards from different sets as a timeline of past, present and future or three different moments in the future.

If you do not feel comfortable with the words on the cards, or the manual of a pack whose pictures you do like, create your own definitions by meditating on each individual card and recording your results so that they become authentic to you. If you don't like any packs, create your own.

FOLLOW-UP ACTIVITIES AND RESEARCH

✧ Create your own tarot layouts, assigning different positions for each card of between four and eleven cards and deciding what the position of each card chosen means for you according to the order it is chosen.

✧ Make your own divinatory set of cards by painting abstract pictures of relevant goddesses or angels on pieces of card. Alternatively, use your own photos and invent a system, maybe roughly based on the tarot.

✧ Invent your own rune-like stones, with magical symbols or astrological signs painted on small pebbles or self-hardening clay.

✧ Expand your knowledge of an existing system, for example the numerological or astrological significance of tarot cards, the meaning of runes both as magical symbols and as a form of esoteric writing.

SEVEN

Moving Beyond Fortune Telling

As clairvoyants we may have to act as life coach to clients and suggest everyday steps necessary to make the desired future possible. For this reason it is a good idea to have an updated list of local advice bureaus, career offices, marriage or child counsellors, addiction centres and even housing and legal associations.

Frustrating though it is, you cannot tell anyone to leave a faithless abusive partner or one who clearly will never commit. Some people will return again and again asking the same questions and still not move forward. All you can do is gently point out the alternatives and use your clairvoyant methods to show that there are other options.

People also come with questions that have a huge amount of emotion attached to them and sometimes heartache behind them. Some are fearful you will deliver bad news so they may be defensive and unresponsive.

HOW TO BE A GOOD CLAIRVOYANT

Listen to what a client is really saying. There may be some uncertainty behind what seems like a straightforward question. You can guide the questioner towards possible practical solutions, for example earning more money through work rather than relying on a lottery win. You should never take away hope: it is a huge responsibility to take away future possibilities and not something I would ever advise, even at the expense of losing credibility.

GETTING THE MOST OUT OF A CLAIRVOYANT SESSION

Firstly explain how you work, what methods you will use and your own beliefs about fate and the future. The difference between fortune telling and clairvoyance is changing the emphasis from telling the client what *will happen* to asking the client *what would you like to happen.*

You can help people to change their lives by showing them a good future they can make through possibilities they had dismissed or of which they had not been aware. Clairvoyance is a wonderful opportunity for the questioner to explore different avenues, especially if you offer a variety of methods in the same reading.

TUNING INTO THE ENERGIES OF OTHER PEOPLE

At the beginning of any session, tune into the aura, or energy field, of the person you are reading for, so that you can understand their hidden feelings and personality.

THE STRUCTURE OF THE AURA

The rainbow-coloured aura or personal energy field that continually flows round us in an ellipse can appear as large as the reach of an extended arm when we are well and happy. If we are exhausted or feeling threatened it will automatically become much smaller. The intensity of the colours indicates whether a person is stressed (radiating harsh shades) or exhausted or lacking confidence (in which case the colours seen will appear pale or even missing in places). You may also notice what look like black knots if there is an ongoing problem. Dark zigzags can be caused by ongoing pressures. You may *see* the aura either externally around the person or in your mind's eye.

The Seven Aura Bands or Divisions

There are seven bands of rainbow colours: red closest to the head and body, then orange, yellow and green. These spiritual energy bands that make up the aura become progressively less dense and more ethereal the further from the physical body they extend. The outer aura levels in blue, indigo/lilac and violet contain the most spiritual energies. Finally, at the outermost limits of the aura, pure white and gold light merge with the cosmos. Often the sixth and seventh indigo/lilac and violet aura levels combine and the outermost layer is perceived as a mixture of violet, gold and white. The coloured rays radiate out in all directions. You may also see pink as part of the green level, brown at the innermost red level and grey that usually acts as an obscuring mist over the whole aura.

Reading the Aura

Two of the aura colour bands, those reflecting the mood and personality of the person being studied, will appear especially vivid and may partially or totally obscure the other colours. These two hold the most useful information in clairvoyant work. The aura is most visible around the head and shoulders, but you can look to either side of your client to avoid staring. If you shake your client's hand or, with someone you know better, hug them, you will also sense the person's current mood and their personality. The mood feels like a bubbly energy and the personality aura is a more slowly throbbing feeling.

The Mood Aura

The mood aura is the predominant aura colour and is constantly moving as it draws from energies around it and also transmits them.

The significance of most colours is self-evident. For example, red is the colour of passion, action, courage or, less positively, anger. However, for fast reference I have put a brief summary of each colour at the end of this chapter and what the harshness or paleness of the shade might indicate.

If you have not read auras before, begin by programming your psychic eye and intuitive senses by saying aloud or in your mind, 'First I wish to focus on the mood aura.' That way your inner intuitive eye will know what to look for, just as when you look at a painting for the first time you focus on the overall impression and only study the details later. After a few sessions you will not need to do this as when you first meet a person the mood aura will appear round them spontaneously.

Slowly close your eyes and then open them, blink and you will *see* the mood aura around the subject, slightly more ethereal than the physical body, like a finely woven curtain. If the aura fades before you have processed the information, repeat the actions and the second time the aura colour/s should remain for longer in your mind or externally.

The Personality Aura

While you were studying the mood aura you may have noticed a background colour. The personality aura is closer to the head than the mood aura and has a more clearly defined shape unless it has been contorted or eroded by trying to please others (a very pale-green lifeless aura).

If you keep looking at the person, the mood aura will fade to form the background and you will notice, quite naturally emerging into the foreground, the personality colour that as the person relaxes with you becomes even more prevalent. This is one reason it is important to relax your client, so initial fear or defensiveness will not obscure their essential personality.

It is in the personality aura you will observe any knots or faded areas.

Understanding the Personality Aura

If you do not see the personality aura, look through half-closed eyes then slowly close your eyes. Open them slowly without blinking.

There is usually one personality colour or there may be a main and also a subsidiary colour. Some people may have two equal colour bands and if these are clear, bright, but not overly harsh this can indicate, for example with green and yellow, someone in whom heart (green) and logic (yellow) are balanced. However, if one or both personality colours are either over-harsh or conversely one very pale, there may be conflicting issues.

Monitoring the Aura During the Session

During the clairvoyant session the mood aura may periodically come to the fore as the questioner starts to feel more positive. Ideally your client will leave with a confident aura (clear orange) or if initially very stressed with a peaceful aura (blue or pink).

For some people their mood aura consistently affects the personality aura in which case the personality aura may remain obscured by or even stained with an overriding mood. If the subject is very resistant to change you may have this problem for a number of subsequent sessions; the problems and the fixed mood may have built up over years.

Aura Problems

The 'block of wood' approach is where a client refuses to fully participate in the session. They may react negatively to whatever you say and there will be a dark-coloured or a grey mood cloud obscuring the aura. The person will be incredibly hard work to read for and it is vital not to become blocked or over-compensate for their lack of enthusiasm by forcing information that does not flow naturally.

✧ Remember they may be deeply unhappy and may not be listening to what you are saying. Suggest they think about your reading and maybe give you some feedback by email if they wish.

✧ Get the client to hold your clear crystal sphere – this may bring some relief and light into their aura (smudge the ball well after the session).

✧ Light a white candle and breathe the light around yourself so you are not adversely affected by the negative aura.

✧ A few clients may demand a free session because they say you have not delivered what they want. If someone will not be helped then you should not feel you have failed.

✧ After such a session either smudge round your head and shoulders, or splash water on your hair, your brow, your throat and your inner wrist pulse points to clear your higher chakras and your aura which may have been drained.

✧ Try to send the difficult client blessings after the session, even if they were rude.

WORKING AS A PROFESSIONAL

✧ Generally thirty minutes is the minimum length of a session. Some people do get very emotional and may need time to compose themselves before feeling ready to go back into the world.

✧ An hour is ideal, but in practice make sessions fifty-five minutes long to allow yourself time to prepare before the next client.

✧ If you are working at a psychic fair you may have to do shorter sessions.

✧ Timekeeping is important. If sessions overrun even by a few minutes, by the end of the day you may be an hour late, which is not fair on other clients.

✧ Equally, if a client is late without prior warning, give a shorter session but charge for the full session.

IF YOU CAN'T FIND ANYTHING DURING A READING

✧ Even the finest clairvoyant or medium has off-days when they get nothing.

✧ If you feel totally blank, stop and hold your crystal ball between your hands to retune into your psychic wavelength while you ask the client some related question. Look for an image in the ball that may open the way into the reading.

✧ It may be that the client is blocking you unconsciously. Explain the alternative meanings of a particular card and ask them to hold the card and say what they see or feel.

✧ Alternatively, switch to another method of divination to shed light, for example a rune or tree stave for each card to expand the meaning.

✧ It may be that there are real contradictions in the person's life. Explain the contradictions you are experiencing in the reading and ask the client why this should be so. They may be relieved to hear that the turmoil is not just in their minds and together you can try to work through the confusion.

✧ If you really cannot get anything from the reading tell the client so and explain this is in no way their fault. Suggest they return another time for a free session, or offer a refund. If you know another practitioner well who uses different methods, say they may be more suited to help them.

✧ If this is happening regularly, you are not losing your abilities, but maybe need a brief rest. Psychic work should always be a pleasure and if you are dreading sessions, you may have problems of your own you need to resolve. Generally a day or two outdoors will restore your enthusiasm.

THE MATTER OF MONEY

There is still the idea that people in clairvoyance should work for free. But you have to eat and pay your electricity bill, so just like any profession you need to set a rate for your time and expertise. Of course you would help someone who had no money and was desperate, but you can only afford to do that if you are charging for the majority of your services. Set a fair price for what you are offering.

Begin with free readings for colleagues, neighbours and friends and then charge a small amount. Once others tell you how accurate you are and friends of friends are asking you for readings, that is the point at which to become a part-time professional.

If you do have extra expertise, have done frequent radio and television clairvoyance work or written books and are well known, set your prices above the average.

ORGANISING YOUR SESSIONS

✧ Make sure you build in short regular breaks for yourself. Drink plenty of water and have a supply of dried fruit, nuts and seeds to keep your blood sugar up.

✧ Ask the client for any specific areas they want to cover so you can organise your time. It is up to you to pace the session so you cover all relevant issues without running over time.

✧ To end a session, start to tidy some cards away while still talking, about five minutes before the end. Say how good it has been to work together and how you are sure things will go well.

✧ If a follow-up session is needed, suggest an appointment in a month's time or maybe after an anticipated major milestone in their lives. For some people one session will be enough.

✧ Sometimes people you have read for will decide to phone you with an update.

✧ Never give out your home or mobile phone number or your private email address.

✧ Display a separate email address and professional mobile or second home phone number on your business card. Keep your answering machine on this number. If a client does contact you and if it is a long or complex matter, suggest they book another session.

✧ If you do work from home, only invite people you know and trust. While you may come to like certain clients, it is import- ant to keep the boundaries of the consultant/client relationship. Occasionally a troubled client can think you are their friend and turn up regularly at your door without warning.

✧ If you suspect a client is mentally troubled, put strict limits on the session and try to guide them towards professional coun- selling or medical care. If you suspect a client is a danger to others, especially a child, then as a last resort contact social ser- vices. This is the only reason for breaking client confidentiality.

FOLLOW-UP ACTIVITIES AND RESEARCH

CREATING A DATABASE

✧ Even if you are working informally with friends and colleagues, start a database with each person's name, personal details and outline of the reading. Try to scribble rough notes as soon after a session as possible and write it up before the memory fades. Note any predictions you made.

✧ When you see the person again or you can monitor your own accuracy, you will notice that you are becoming increasingly accurate and this in its turn gives you the confidence to say things that may seem to make no sense at the time of the session, but subsequently do happen.

✧ You may notice that in a subsequent reading the same cards appear or perhaps those that do turn up are the natural progression.

✧ As you read for more and more people it is all too human to forget details, but try to recall where a client was on their life path last time you met and the names of relevant people in their life (the beauty of keeping a database).

AURA COLOURS

Use the definitions below as the basis for your own colour meanings, using books and online resources and aura readings you do to build up your own detailed aura colour chart.

Red: Movement, courage, change, passion and physical strength, action, determination; less positively, anger, lust, stubbornness, suppressed resentment and a desire to bully or dominate.

Orange: Confidence, joy, creativity, fertility, abundance and independence; less positively, unsociability, eccentricity, addictiveness or lack of self-esteem.

Yellow: Logic, focus, financial acumen, technological expertise, adaptability, a traveller; less positively, spite, jealousy or emotional coldness.

Green: Love, fidelity, loyalty, a lover of beauty and nature, good luck, a healer, sympathetic; less positively, possessiveness, overdependency on others and sentimentality.

Blue: Justice, idealism, acquired or traditional knowledge, harmony with others, wise leadership and an ability to see both sides of the question; less positively, over-concern with rules and regulations or an inability to make a decision.

Purple: Imagination, spiritual powers, the sign of a natural psychic, a seeker after truth, ability to always see the best in others and any situation, a visionary; less positively, someone who is totally unrealistic and lives in a dream or fantasy world.

Pink: A peacemaker and natural healer of sorrows, animals and children, one who cares for others and nurtures them; less positively, over-anxiety, a martyr and an inability to defend anyone or any principle.

Brown: Stability, security, reliability, a practical trustworthy person who is good with money and details; less positively, someone who is mean, over-materialistic or totally overburdened by life.

Grey: Compromise, tact, adaptability and the ability to keep a low profile; less positively, over-secrecy, maybe a double life or unwillingness to commit to others.

EIGHT

Clairvoyance and Other Dimensions

WORKING WITH PAST LIVES: WHAT IS KNOWN AND IS IT REAL?

Even if the idea of past lives seems improbable to you, we know that modern human beings are descended from a common genetic source. Therefore, because we share the same heritage, it may be possible for people to access a universal past. From this we can recall memories of lives that share similarities to our own or those of our ancestors.

WHY PRACTISE PAST LIVES?

Past-life experiences can help us to understand seemingly illogical fears and phobias and this can be very healing in our present lives and even explain why certain psychic powers seem blocked. Past-life work is extremely valuable to see recurring patterns from previous lives and how a client can make necessary changes. Equally, a person can understand through past-life work how a current relationship that is proving destructive can be linked to a past-life experience.

One theory is that we travel through different lifetimes with a family of souls who may assume different roles in subsequent lives. A twin soul with whom you have a passionate instinctive connection may not always feature in a lifetime as lasting love or a lifelong partner but may be a brother, mother, or if a lover the relationship may be cut short or not develop till later in life.

Generally you will identify at least three or four core souls plus maybe the twin soul which could even manifest as intense dislike turning rapidly to passion in subsequent lives. You can follow a single past-life recall with clairvoyant methods into future pathways, using the information gained in the past life.

UNDERSTANDING YOUR OWN PAST WORLDS

There may be a particular period to which you feel instinctively connected, perhaps have dreamed about frequently, or felt at home when you visited another part of the world. If no special location calls you, visit different ancient sites, ruined abbeys, cathedrals and churches, industrial museums, old stone circles or the sites of temples, reconstructed villages with authentic buildings, folklore centres, castles and cathedrals. War museums and battlefields, because of the great loss of life in dramatic circumstances, often trigger remembrances. Do this also on holidays and days out. Every country has heritage sites that recall the past and often contain artefacts you can handle.

TUNING INTO PAST LIVES IN HISTORIC PLACES

✧ To establish or speed up your own past-life links, go to a chosen site either very early or late in the day when the light is soft and it is quiet.

✧ Find an old doorway and slowly walk through, picturing a thin mist or soft curtain. Blink, and you may see for a moment the place as it was in a period that relates to you, even if the specific place has no actual connection with your past life.

You are using the doorway as a time portal to trigger a similar experience.

✧ Close your eyes and use your fingertips and palms to make connection with walls, statues, artefacts and furniture.

✧ If you are not allowed to touch anything, extend your hands palms vertically facing outwards, as close to the item as you can and imagine you are warming your hands by a fire. You can connect with the energy field of an object even through glass.

✧ Still with closed eyes allow a person to form in your mind from another time or place holding a similar item or standing in a similar place. Then as you open your eyes slowly you may get a momentary shadowy glimpse of an outline and feel tremendous warmth as you see yourself as you were.

✧ If there is a mirror in the room, position yourself so you cannot see your own reflection. Look at the reflected scene behind you.

✧ Only if you are ready, look into the mirror at your face as it is, blink and you may see yourself in the past world.

✧ Move away, sit in a quiet spot and allow any memories to return of people or locations. You may identify people you knew in that life, maybe in similar situations.

✧ When the life fades, send a blessing to yourself as you once were. Before leaving, cleanse your energy field (as before) and say, 'Let me take with me what is of use to my present path. I leave the rest where it belongs to trouble me no more.'

✧ Further details may emerge spontaneously or in dreams. Check any details against what is known. If a particular site or artefact triggers rich past-life memories, return at different times of the day and in different seasons.

WAYS OF WORKING WITH THE PAST LIVES OF YOURSELF AND OTHERS

Experiencing Past Dimensions using Psychometric Transfer

You can use an authentic reproduction of an ancient artefact as a channel or doorway to take you into the past. You can then transfer the associations generated by the artefact to a former life when you or a client used a similar artefact or lived or worked in a similar place.

✧ Collect a series of authentic items or lovingly crafted reproduction items to trigger recall in others. On my Scandinavian travels I have collected a Viking wise woman staff, a bronze pendant of the Norse goddess Freya in her falcon headed form, and a spear of the Father God Odin. I also have genuine Navajo animal and bird fetishes, a selection of animal horns from different ages and cultures, a Peruvian fertility doll, African animal and human wooden statues and clay water bottles, Baltic shamanic charms and Ancient Egyptian, Hindu and Chinese artefacts. I ask clients or groups I am teaching to hold them in turn and see if they feel affinity to any of them. Collect items on holidays and from garage sales, ethnic Fair Trade stores, from indigenous online traders or antique markets. The more extensive your collection the more effective the method.

✧ Light a candle and work in darkness. Ask a client to describe their feelings as they hold a chosen item, what they see and feel, and to picture themselves holding or using the item in a particular world.

✧ Sometimes a seemingly unrelated item can act as a doorway across cultures. For example, my Viking wise woman staff has several times put members of a class in touch with past worlds in which they were apprenticed to Native North American medicine men and women, while the bull horn is a direct link to the world of the Celts, and especially the Druid priest-hood.

USING CRYSTALS

✧ Use your clear crystal sphere for past lives, especially in sunlight. You need marks and cracks inside so you can identify figures. You can hold darker crystal spheres like amethyst and smoky quartz to candlelight or moonlight. Alternatively, focus on a crystal pyramid with markings inside, especially in the squat shape like the Giza pyramids. These are believed to transmit clairvoyant energies and have been shown to spontaneously encourage light trance states.

✧ In any of these look for a figure that will often seem to be moving and will be unusually sharp in focus. The figure will be distinctly dressed and carrying something and if you keep looking in the same place, you will notice more detail, as though you were looking at a tiny moving screen.

✧ Start to talk about the figure aloud and as you keep looking at the same place the scene will evolve.

✧ A client may, if you show them the images you see, add details and then begin to take over and describe the scene.

✧ The person seeing the past life will relate to the details of the life and character and you can ask them to pick up to six tarot cards afterwards to clarify the experience.

Gateway Crystals

Crystals with a deep indentation such as agate, citrine or amethyst geode-like caves, as well as blue celestine eggs with holes, offer phys-ical doorways. Transparent quartz crystals, called phantom quartz, have another shadowy half-formed crystal inside that looks like a doorway. If you shine a small tea light on the entrance within the crystal you can create a flickering doorway of light. Alternatively, shine a small tea light on the surface of an opaque pyramid and use that as an entrance – talk your client through the doorway and beyond with guided visualisation.

USING FRAGRANCES TO REACH PAST WORLDS THROUGH CLAIRSENTIENCE

Natural fragrances can be used either alone or in conjunction with any of the past-life methods described in this chapter. Check a client is not allergic to smoke or any particular fragrances. The principle is that the fragrance acts as a time channel to an earlier life when the person previously smelled the fragrance. Effective past-life fragrances include cedar, cinnamon, copal, cypress, frank-incense, hibiscus, honeysuckle, hyacinth, jasmine, juniper, lavender, lemon, lilac, lotus, orange, sweet marjoram, mimosa, mint, myrrh, papyrus flower, rose, sage, thyme and sandalwood.

You can also for personal exploration use smells such as baking bread, roasting meat, beeswax furniture polish, wood smoke, starch, tar, pine forests, the sea, or go into a rose garden or fields of lavender and herbs.

Traditionally juniper, cedar and sandalwood are burned on a fire to induce past-life experiences sent, it is said, by the Archangel Azrael, but you can also burn them as mixed oils or incenses as a stimulus.

Light a candle, unless you are using a scented candle as the main stimulus. Beeswax, rose and lavender candles are very effective for past-life recall. Sprinkle a few grains of dried lavender or thyme in the candle flame and ask that you or the client be shown the life that has most to tell you about the present situation. Inhale a fragrance through cologne, perfume, incense or oil, or burn a scented candle. Alternatively, try a naturally occurring fragrance outdoors: for example, standing in a market that sells fruits, flowers and spices. If you close your eyes the sounds of the vendors may also carry you back to other marketplaces.

Count softly from twenty down to one and ask the person where they are now as they smell the fragrance. If they say, for example, they are smelling a rose bush, ask them where the bush is and then perhaps lead them out of the garden, gently prompting them, until they are talking spontaneously.

PREPARING FOR A PAST-LIFE SESSION

The aim is to create a light trance state so that from visualising a doorway the mind switches to actually experiencing the past world.

Reassure a client that nothing bad can happen, that you will be with them all the time and that if they wish to return you will guide them back instantly. For some people the experience is emotional because the release of blocked feelings often proves very healing.

The following are stages to guide someone into the past. Practise recording the steps on a cassette with pauses so you can learn the sequence by heart. Create your own scenarios that work well for you and your clients.

◇ Work somewhere quiet where the client can relax and take off their shoes. Somewhere warm but not too hot. Draw the curtains and light a candle and some incense. Make sure you will not be interrupted.

◇ Use a relaxation method if a person seems tense or is new to psychic work. Suggest the person close their eyes. My favourite relaxation technique is imagining a butterfly landing on various parts of the body. The person holds that part motionless while the butterfly rests there and then relaxes as the butterfly moves upwards.

◇ Next, describe a place of beauty such as a garden with a flight of steps down and as part of the visualisation, count the client down the steps from twenty to one.

✧ Describe a scene for the client to visualise: the entrance to a crystal cave through which they walk towards a point of light; a boat on a river that will gently float to a landing stage; a magic carpet ride through the stars. Assess what would work best for the client, but avoid anything dark, too enclosed or uncertain.

✧ Then describe a stage of transition: walking through a doorway or a curtain of golden light; walking over a bridge from the landing stage into bright light.

✧ Play soft background music or gently sound a bell to mark moving into the other world.

✧ To identify who they are, start by asking them to visualise who they are at five years old. Tell them to look down at the feet, the ground and then their clothes. If they cannot see, ask if they can hear or sense anything. Encourage the person to keep talking.

✧ Then someone calls them as they are too young to be out alone. Someone coming to take them home. Identify the person and where home is.

✧ In their home, ask them to focus on an object, then widen the view around the home or look out of a window. Ask who else is present and what is happening and how they feel.

✧ Then count through softly and slowly, year by year, to ten years old. Ask if they are still in the same place and if anyone is missing or there are additions to the family.

✧ Keep moving forward in five-year stages. If you come to a significant event, for example a pregnancy, a wedding, or going to war, you can move forward more slowly.

✧ If at some point the person cannot see anything after moving forward they may have died or undergone a traumatic event. Explain they seem to have died and give them the option of leaving the life and you filling them in later. Some people do not want to see the death, but assure them that they will not experience it, just see a picture.

✧ Now count very slowly back from twenty, picking up the experience of the steps. It is not usually necessary to retrace the whole journey. On five say, 'You will now become aware of the room and the sounds of the everyday world again.' On one say, 'Open your eyes whenever you feel ready.'

✧ Sit quietly in the candlelight. Allow the client to talk about the experience, identify any people who feature in this world and to make connections with any past and present traumas.

✧ If necessary find two or three crystal ball images to expand the experience and offer any suggestions for applying the new insights to the present situation.

ASTRAL PROJECTION

Astral projection – also known as out-of-body experiences, etheric or spirit body travel – refers to the sensation of floating or flying while the physical body remains inert. To many indigenous peoples throughout the world, astral projection is a reality both in sleep and during waking hours.

No one can be sure whether the person is travelling in their mind (remote viewing) or their inner, almost-identical spiritual body actually leaves the physical body for a while. Witnesses describe how during an out-of-body experience the physical body of the astral traveller seems lifeless and quite floppy. It is very easy and safe to learn how to travel astrally, and useful for personal development.

WHERE YOU CAN GO ON YOUR ASTRAL TRAVELS

✧ To other people's homes: if you know the place well look for a new feature that has been added since you last visited.

✧ Unfamiliar locations you're going to in the near future. Again, look for unfamiliar and distinctive landmarks you can verify.

✧ A distant land you have always wanted to see: stand in a marketplace, rainforest or cathedral and saviour the atmosphere. Recall the route or unusual hidden features and check your accuracy either online or during a future visit if you record the details.

✧ Travel to the land of your ancestors, either where they once actually lived or where they are now in the afterlife. You will find that they are living in a place remarkably similar to where they were most happy in this life, and in ways not so very different, except that they will appear young and healthy. You may see them as if through a glass window or a screen, but you can speak to them and they may give you a message.

✧ Visit your guardian angels and spirit guides in their own realms or maybe experience the former earthly life of a current wise spiritual guide when you lived together in an ancient world.

✧ Sit outdoors in a green place and travel to the realms of the nature spirits.

✧ Go to the stars and explore the universe.

✧ Visit future lovers or people you are not in contact with in daily life, either in a dream or in a very relaxed state just before or after sleep.

Crystals for Astral Projection: Amber, yellow, peach, green, blue or white calcite, carnelian, jet, haematite, Herkimer diamond, black onyx, golden topaz or black and white tourmalated quartz.
Astral travel fragrances: Basil, frankincense, freesia, jasmine, mugwort, sandalwood, or the all-purpose lavender and rose.

HOW TO EXPERIENCE ASTRAL PROJECTION

Initially you may need to deliberately visualise each of the stages, but before long it will happen spontaneously. Choose a time where you can be uninterrupted for at least thirty minutes.

✧ In advance, switch on a lamp on top of a wardrobe or a high shelf, or focus on lit candles in a high wall bracket. In either case you should lie in the opposite corner of the room from the source of light so you can easily look up at it.

✧ Light one of the astral fragrances, and if after dark light a purple or silver candle (as well as the astral ones). Soft sunlight or shimmering moonlight are also good backgrounds for journeys.

✧ Play very slow, soft music to screen out any disruptive sounds.

✧ Lie with your head propped up on a sofa, bed or cushions so that you are totally comfortable and your spine is straight and you can comfortably look up at the light.

✧ Ask your guardian angel or wise spirit to protect you as you travel through other realms and to bring you home safely.

✧ Picture yourself surrounded by white light.

✧ Breathe slowly, deeply and regularly through your diaphragm and push away any irrelevant thoughts or worries.

✧ Hold an astral crystal in each hand (two different colours) to make a spiritual link through your palm chakras.

✧ Looking up at the light, breathe in gently and then exhale. With each inhaled breath, draw the light all around you and picture the light getting larger as you start to move towards it.

✧ Starting with one, still breathing gently and slowly, count aloud as though walking up diagonal steps of light and suddenly you will find that you have a sensation of floating rather than climbing. Do not look down.

✧ When you are surrounded by the light and have the sensation of being high up, move around, either standing vertically as though you are walking on air, or floating horizontally as though swimming in water. Enjoy the sensation.

✧ If in a small room with a low ceiling practise floating out through an open door and moving round the house or even outdoors by imagining a wall melting and becoming a curtain of light.

✧ When you feel ready, move downwards again counting backwards and when you reach the ground, hug your body and you will experience a warm liquid sensation as your two bodies, spiritual and physical, merge.

MOVING TO OTHER DIMENSIONS

Practise this outdoors if possible and then you can more easily visualise the experiences.

✧ On a clear night, lie or sit under a tall tree and look up through the branches so you can see a single star directly above you.

✧ Picture a silver cord extending from your navel like a rope or ladder of light, attached at the other end to the top of the tree and then extending as a spiralling light path upwards towards the stars.

✧ Half-close your eyes and focus on a star that is especially bright.

✧ Breathe slowly and regularly. In your imagination, gently draw the starlight towards you with each breath so that the star expands and moves closer as you climb.

✧ Each time you breathe out, slowly push your inner astral self up vertically as though you were casting off weights that were holding you down. In your mind's vision extend your arms like wings. Count up from one to thirty if it helps.

✧ Picture the silver light all around you and then identify a door in the light that looks black. In fact it is open and as you float through it you enter the universe of stars and velvet darkness.

✧ Now the cosmos is yours to explore: visit past worlds, the realms of the ancestors, other places in this world, other universes or call your twin soul.

✧ When you want to come home, enter a door in any bright star and float gently down a spiral counting back from thirty until you are on the ground again.

✧ Sit quietly and let the star light recede slowly. Gradually let the scenes unfold as you recall your magical journey.

✧ You can recreate this sensation indoors using twinkling Christmas lights, draped high up in a corner of the room, a small fibre optic tree on a tall shelf, or neon ceiling stars. Alternatively, practise in a planetarium during a show.

PROGRESSION OR EXPLORING FUTURE LIVES

You can travel as far ahead in the future as you wish, though what you see are only future possibilities. You can explore your future in this life, but you will never see your death as that is not fixed. If you experience a blank it does not mean you have died, merely that the information has yet to be formed.

You can also use future life exploration, with great care, for other people. You can comfortably explore up to twenty or even thirty years ahead (according to the age of the client) by using cards or a crystal ball, one image or card for each five-year increment (or yearly if preferred). Many people do fear old age and a positive reading can be very reassuring and empowering.

PROGRESSIONS USING VISUALISATION

This is for clients who are curious about future lives or their descendants. The time frame is up to the client, but suggest moving forward 100 years from now, then 150, then 200 years and as far forward as they wish. Some people naturally see personal events linked with the future of the family, but others link into more global events.

SUGGESTED TECHNIQUES FOR EXPLORING PERSONAL FUTURE LIVES

Whatever method you use you need, as with past lives, to pass into another dimension. This time it is more like crossing an unbroken horizon from night to day on a long plane journey or climbing a hill on a misty day and seeing the world below spread out as the mist clears.

✧ Use any of the relaxation and visualisation techniques previously suggested, but this time guide the client to ascend steps into brilliant light, walk up a hill or make horizontal steps across the sky from night to day, counting slowly from one to twenty until the vista stretches open ahead or below from the hilltop showing a future scene.

✧ Begin by saying, 'What you see is a hundred years from now.' You will see what your client sees, so help them to interpret the scene by questioning them about their vision though you are sharing it.

✧ When it feels that all relevant has been seen, describe mist falling and count forward in fives until you reach 150 years ahead where the clouds clear to show the next point in time. It can be possible to identify oneself in a future life by feeling a warm connection as in past worlds. Explain this in advance.

✧ Continue moving forward until you sense the connection fading or the client does not wish to progress further. Then start the descent from twenty to one on which the present returns.

✧ Thank the guardians who have walked through time with you.

✧ It can be helpful to use the crystal ball to identify some of the most relevant scenes or even tarot cards or animal cards, one for each image.

FOLLOW-UP ACTIVITIES AND RESEARCH

CHANNELLING WISDOM ABOUT THE FUTURE FROM ANGELS, SPIRIT GUIDES AND WISE TEACHERS

Stage 1

✧ You will need to use your clear crystal pendulum as a channel and an amplifier.

✧ Light a white candle and any floral incense or oil that is especially potent for angelic connections. Soft background music may also stimulate clairaudience.

✧ Hold the pendulum in the hand you write with and put the other cupped hand round it so your palm chakra is connecting with the pendulum vibrations, but not touching the pendulum.

✧ Always ask to be surrounded by love and light and that only those with good intention and the highest goodness speak with you.

✧ You can ask a particular guide to work with you or request the wise guide or angel who can be of most help to you. When working with clients you can connect and communicate with their guides, angels or ancestors if you hold the pendulum in this way as you talk to the client.

✧ Wait until you feel the pendulum vibrating and the same sensation in your palm. You may see, hear or feel the guide either externally or usually, at first, in your mind.

✧ Then ask a question of the guide: about their life or messages they may have for you about the future, or you can ask a client's guides what they wish to say to the client about their future life.

✧ Keep seeking information until you sense the connection fading.

✧ Thank the guardian and say, 'Go in peace and blessings till we meet again.' Blow out the candle to break the connection.

Stage 2: Developing personal channelling abilities for future guidance

Each time you ask a question about the future and have received an answer, transfer the pendulum to the other hand and, using a green-ink pen and cream paper, write down the answers. An angel, guide or ascended being will be guiding your hand. If you allow the questions to come spontaneously, the guardian will, in time, channel a great deal of wisdom that will guide you to the right places and reveal to you the skills you need to learn to make that future more golden and to use your gifts more widely.

Stage 3: Prophecy

Now you are ready to try prophecy, drawing from the cosmic well of wisdom and the guardians of time, to discover what may come to pass. This time you will use only your pen and paper and the candle, and the future revealed will be less personal and more global. Ask that you may know what is hidden, which could be revealed for the benefit of others.

Keep a special book for this channelling and look at the candle until you feel moved to write. Write until you feel no more will come. Give thanks to the guardians of time who have allowed you to see what is right to be known. By candlelight, read what you have written which may be a poem, a story or a lot of symbols that you will need to meditate on. Blow out the candle. Repeat the process and over the months you will develop your own book of future wisdom. Some may be specific predictions, almost always about global rather than personal events, but others will be long-ranging prophecies. You may wish to publish these online or as a book.

NINE

Clairvoyance and Ghosts

As a clairvoyant you will see ghosts everywhere. Invariably you will be asked for advice on identifying other people's ghosts, or even be asked to remove a paranormal presence that may be frightening a family member, albeit unintentionally. The identification and removal of workplace ghosts is frequently undertaken by clairvoyants.

Though we hear most about ghosts of battlefields or those who died dramatically, by far the majority of ghosts lived ordinary lives. Sometimes ghosts choose to remain in a house where they were happy and died in their own beds after a long uneventful life. Indeed, for every so-called restless spirit trapped and unable to move on are a thousand more that have a good reason and want to be in the place they are sighted.

Some ghosts you encounter may be deceased family members come back to peep into the cradle of a newborn or to celebrate a family wedding, as they would have done in life. Once you explain this, a worried family may welcome their household guardian. A noisy household presence may be a resident of earlier days who may still tidy up at night (often mistaken for a nasty ghost because they clatter around when the house is quiet). Of course there are unfriendly ghosts, for I believe that if people were nasty in life, death is unlikely to improve them. Such bad tempered or unhappy souls may feel unable to move on from the earth plane. Some, it seems, are so wrapped up in their own selfishness, they do not realise they are dead. They are not dangerous, just a nuisance and if you encounter one away from the home they are best left alone.

APPARITIONS

Apparitions are attached to a specific place or artefact (such as a wedding ring). They may be seen or sensed by different people over a number of years or even centuries. They seem unaware that they are being perceived and are like a photographic impression etched on the energy field or aura of a location. These apparitions may have been originally imprinted by strong emotion at the time of the person's death, either because of a great trauma or a great happiness on that spot. Ghosts of monks, nuns and servants who spent their whole lives carrying out repetitive actions may also become part of a collective aura or energy field and for this reason many abbeys and former monasteries are haunted.

We activate these ghosts by entering their space and then sounds and images will unfold before us. Anniversaries of a battle seem to prompt a lot of ghost sightings even from people who had no knowledge of the significance of the event. But any place where many people lived or worked over a long period of time is a good source of apparitions for practise if you are new to ghost work.

PARANORMAL PRESENCES

Ghosts that are presences interact with, or at least seem aware of, observers, suggesting the survival of the essential person. They either choose to stay in, or feel unable to leave, a location that was of significance during earthly life. It may be they are perceived on a particular anniversary or return periodically to appear at the time of a family celebration to give advice and comfort.

It is sometimes said that we are all spirits within an earthly body. Indeed many researchers into spiritual energies believe that we possess within our physical body a spirit double or etheric body. This is hypothesised to be the part of us, our essential soul, that survives after death. It has been described clairvoyantly and also by children either as a silver essence or a double of our physical body at its peak. For this reason a returning relative tends to look in good health and much younger than the time of death. During life our own spiritual double may be seen occasionally going walk-about by an independent observer while we are asleep or travelling in our mind.

INVESTIGATING GHOSTLY PRESENCES OR APPARITIONS

In recent years, technology has enabled ghost investigators to assess the physical effects of the presence of an apparition using instruments to measure magnetic fields, and infrared thermometers to record temperatures where the ghostly presences are detected. But even the most high-tech investigation relies on clairvoyants to interpret the findings and to identify and sometimes communicate with the ghosts. Indeed, you can see and identify ghosts with nothing more elaborate than a crystal pendulum and your evolving psychic senses.

The following is a useful checklist for paranormal investigations.

Is there really a presence or do the apparently paranormal noises have a more earthly cause such as faulty plumbing? A paranormal energy feels like ripples of air, but colder and more fluid. Human energies are much more solid and heavy since they are rooted in the earth. The cold spot where a ghost sits or stands feels like someone leaving the front door open in a house on a chilly day, as air rushes in from the parting of the dimensions. Even an apparition gives off this light, cold energy.

The difference between a presence and an apparition is the difference between seeing a person on a film or on a web camera: the person on camera is actually connecting with you even if they are not speaking. Knowing instinctively whether the spirit is an apparition or presence becomes automatic with practice.

Can you smell any fragrances, such as lavender or pipe tobacco, and at the same time feel as though the hairs are prickling on the back of your neck?

This may indicate the presence of a spirit who used the fragrance in life. If a relative, the house owner may immediately identify the ghost, having previously thought they were imagining the smell.

Was the paranormal activity triggered by any special event such as redecoration? Were any old items found or do any items belonging to a deceased family member seem to prompt paranormal happenings?

If so, hold these items and see if you can feel a sense of the presence hovering around as if to say, 'Hey, that's mine, leave it alone.' The energies emanating from the object will be quite sparky, almost like a mild electric shock, if the former owner is still around.

Can you feel a ghost path?

Through the small chakras in the sole of each foot, you will pick up psychometric information as you walk a path which ghosts walked during their earthly lives and may still walk after death. The information about the ghost is impressed into the floor and a still-active ghost path will give off a strong buzzing. The impressions left by a ghost no longer present will feel lighter, but still tingly. Use a pendulum to help you tune into the path.

When you reach the path, the pendulum will spiral in a clockwise swing and you will feel a vibration up the chain and into your fingers. The intensity of the vibrations will indicate if a ghost is still using the path. When you encounter the outer limits of the aura space of the actual ghost (like the living aura, about an extended arm span in diameter, but more ethereal in texture), the pendulum will vibrate very strongly and may be hard to control.

Can you hear sounds: voices, music, machinery, singing or shouting? Is there anything in the voice – a particular song, a turn of phrase or an accent that might identify the ghost to the person who lives in the house?

Visit the building when it's quiet and switch on a tape recorder if you wish. Though a tape may pick up sounds if left overnight, the presence of a clairvoyant evokes more response. If you hear anything unusual, ask locals for information. If someone died in the house, an elderly neighbour might recall details, for example if a former resident had a Welsh accent or played the flute.

What can you see?

From the ghost seekers' point of view, actually seeing a ghost will provide clues that enable the apparition to be easily identified either as belonging to a particular period in time or nationality, or as a known relative or former resident.

Occasionally a ghost may appear totally solid and three-dimensional. However, some ghosts, especially those that are apparations rather than true presences, are seen like a black and white photographic image or mist. Some people only see part of a ghost or a misty outline, if the apparition does not have the force to fully manifest itself. If you cannot see anything but are sure there is a presence, focus on the area where you sense the presence is and try to feel the spherical aura limits, like a very light resistance. Stare hard and you will detect a faint shimmer of light in the centre. Relax your eyes and slowly the form will take shape. Keep your focus as steady as possible and do not move as the presence manifests. It may at first only appear for a moment but if you blink and then look at the same spot it will come back into vision. An apparition may speak but only have one or two key phrases, frozen in the atmosphere.

CREATING A FRIENDLY ENCOUNTER WITH A PRESENCE

Forming a friendly relationship with a ghost who is actually sentient is important. A presence still emits an aura that interacts directly with that of living people and can hold a telepathic communication (or very rarely a physical conversation).

✧ Stop about an arm's length in front of the ghost so you do not intrude on its space.

✧ Smile and greet the ghost in your mind, or aloud if alone.

✧ The presence may turn and go away, in which case do not follow. However, usually the ghost will smile back and may show you images in your mind of their former life or communicate words you will hear in your mind or externally.

✧ Some are eager to share their life story and if an injustice has been done, being acknowledged may be enough to bring the ghost peace.

✧ Listen to their message and when the encounter fades say, 'Go in peace and blessings to your world with thanks as I go back to mine.'

✧ There might be a sudden chill as the ghost returns to his or her dimension.

✧ Turn away, leave the place and as you go out through the entrance, splash a little water (from a small bottle you should carry) on your brow and say, 'The connection between us is cut with blessings.'

✧ Do not take anything away from the house as you may disturb the natural vibrations. The phantom has no interest in leaving its home and following you. If you do ever feel spooked, turn and, from a small container you should carry, drop salt behind you, saying, 'Return to your world as I do to mine.'

EXTRA PSYCHIC PROTECTION DURING WORK WITH GHOSTS

✧ You might like to carry a tiny crystal angel or wear one on a chain when you explore paranormal energies.

✧ Alternatively, wear a small cross that you have sprinkled with mineral water in which three pinches of salt were dissolved. You can anoint your angel in the same way.

✧ Before you begin, say a silent prayer asking that your special angel, your god/goddess or the power of light will enfold you in protection.

✧ Before dealing with a difficult ghost, find a quiet place, touch your hairline and say, 'Above me the light.' Then touch the centre of your brow and say, 'Before me the radiance.' Touch your throat, saying, 'Protected may I be.' Finally, touch your heart and say, 'Safe within the Light of Love.'

✧ If you get the feeling that the energies are menacing, walk away at once after saying, 'Go in peace and blessing.' Walk away just as you would from a living person who wasn't friendly.

DEALING WITH PROBLEMATIC GHOSTS

Generally you are invited to deal with a ghost because they are causing difficulties to living residents or scaring people in a house or workplace. They might not be malicious but merely noisy, over-curious about the current inhabitants or eager to restore things as they were, if there have been renovations.

✧ Begin by asking the house owner where the ghostly presence is felt and confirm this for yourself.

✧ Even if you are an experienced clairvoyant, the idea of exorcism is best left in the Middle Ages. A spirit may either want to stay or be totally confused and not realise he or she has died. Gentleness and kindness work best and if there is an angry spirit, casting him or her out is only likely to provoke an even angrier reaction.

✧ Try the following method and if it doesn't work, use further methods and visit more frequently. But leave time for things to settle down as it can take a few days for energies to restore to normal even if you have removed the problem.

✧ Totally evil spirits are very rare. Sometimes if people have been playing about with a ouija board or amateur séances, people can call unintelligent spirits, like the yobs of the paranormal world, that can pretend to be all kinds of things and cause energies to pop light bulbs or even shatter glass. Often people have frightened themselves and may be releasing their own energy as poltergeist – or uncontrolled psychokinetic – activity rather than having released a spirit.

✧ Again check if there is actually a presence causing the disturbances, even if you do not witness them. Even an apparently malevolent poltergeist can be caused by a psychically sensitive teenager, channelling collective family stress.

✧ If you sense this, do not identify the teenager as this can create a scapegoat for what is a family problem or make them worry that the child is possessed by evil spirits. In this case, suggest counselling for the family or practical solutions to problems and perform a simple blessing as though there were a poltergeist.

HELPING A PRESENCE TO MOVE ON

✧ Give the owner the option of being present so you can act as an intermediary in any dialogue with the spirit, or report your findings to them later.

✧ On a central table in the room where the haunting is most prevalent, light four white or beeswax candles and place them at three, six, nine and twelve on an imaginary clock face. These represent the four protective archangels.

✧ In the centre of the table set a bowl of fragrant dried flower petals or a floral pot pourri.

✧ Sit quietly at the table and say softly, 'Friend, you are welcome. I wish to know who you are and why you are here.'

✧ If you sense hostility, set a clove of garlic or dish of salt in the centre of the table also. Sit quietly and wait until you feel the presence and perhaps see a figure materialising. The reason for the spirit being there will become clear, either as a telepathic communication or as impressions or images. If it is a sad reason you can ask the ghost if they would like help in moving on to where they will be happy. But sometimes acknowledging their reason from the past for being angry or sad acts as a release as they feel your sympathy.

✧ Courteously explain to the ghost any problems he or she may be unknowingly causing. Explain to the presence that while the owner is happy to share the home, they should try not to disturb the current residents.

✧ Gently explain that their earthly life is over and that there are friends and relatives waiting for them in the afterlife. If they look straight ahead they will see a beautiful light into which they can walk. You will see this light. Describe the people waiting to re-assure the ghost.

✧ If they do go you will feel the presence leave the room like a light going out.

✧ If the spirit chooses to stay as a guardian or after he or she has departed, pick up one of the candles and carry it clockwise around the room into the four corners, beginning nearest the door saying, 'Go to the light or stay in the light of the world with peace and blessings.'

✧ Repeat with the other three candles.

✧ Then take the first candle into every room and standing in the centre say, 'Go in peace to the light or stay in peace with blessings in the light of the world.'

✧ Return the candle and leave them to burn through.

IF THE PARANORMAL ACTIVITY CONTINUES

Should your initial visit not produce the desired results after a few days and the ghost is still present and noisy or causing fear, you need to repeat the blessings using extra and more powerful methods.

✧ Light a tall gold or natural beeswax candle in the middle of a small central table in the room where the paranormal activity is most felt.

✧ Lift the candle as you stand in the middle of the room facing the main door and then carry it into the four corners in turn, beginning with the one nearest the door and moving anti-clockwise, seeing if you can link into the ghostly energies; do not deliberately make contact this time.

✧ Say in the centre and when you visit each corner, 'May only goodness, light and peace remain here. Go, now, to where you belong, for your loved ones are waiting.'

✧ When you have visited all four corners return to the centre of the room, raise the candle again and revisit the four corners, this time in clockwise order. Repeat the words.

✧ Next ring a small bell (a crystal or metal hand bell, or Tibetan bells) three times in the centre of the room, facing the main door, and then in the four corners, again moving anticlockwise, ringing it once in each corner. After ringing the bell in each place, say again, 'May only goodness, light and peace remain here. Go now to where you belong for your loved ones are waiting.'

✧ Return to the centre, ring the bell thee times again, still facing the door, and then move clockwise ringing the bell in each of the four corners, repeating the words.

✧ Now light an incense stick from the candle flame in a protective fragrance such as rose, sage, frankincense, juniper, lemon, lemongrass, lilac, lily of the valley, myrrh, orange, patchouli or pine.

✧ Facing the door, raise the incense stick upwards in the centre and then walk round the four corners of the room anticlockwise, making anticlockwise spirals in the air as you walk with the stick in the hand you write with. Keep saying the same words as before in the centre and each corner to imprint them.

✧ Then return to the centre and, walking clockwise this time, repeat the words and movements in all four corners till you are back in the centre.

✧ Return the incense to the table.

✧ This time blow out the candle and say, 'Go now to the light in peace to your own place and find happiness once more.'

✧ The extinguishing candle flame will help to generate the light into which the spirit will travel.

✧ If other rooms or areas are affected you can visit them at every stage with the same candle, bell and incense and follow the same procedure. Relight the candle in each new room.

IF YOU STILL SENSE THE PRESENCE

Return after a few days if there are still problems.

✧ Add a few pinches of ordinary sea salt to a bowl of water from a tap that has been left running so the water sparkles.

◇ Stir the water three times clockwise with a silver knife and then make a cross on the surface of the water, asking for blessings on the affected home or workplace.

◇ Light a white candle in the room most room affected.

◇ Sprinkle a few drops of salt water in the four corners of the room, this time moving only clockwise.

◇ Say in the room before you leave. 'Go from this place all that is sad, that is not beautiful and of this earth. You, departed friend, are no longer of this earth and now must move to where you can receive peace and healing.' Blow out the candle in that room.

◇ If you want to protect the whole house, mix a larger quantity of salt water in a bigger bowl. Light a different small white candle in each room affected and scatter circles of salt water in the corners as you walk from the front of the house to the back, top to bottom and in the corner of each room. Repeat the blessing words in each room and area, and blow out the candle in each room before leaving it.

◇ Throw any leftover salt water out of the front door or tip it down a drain outside.

◇ In any area where you still sense an unfriendly paranormal presence or atmosphere, after doing the above, sprinkle sea salt over the threshold of the internal doors of any room or rooms affected and on the external main back and front doorsteps.

◇ Change the blessing words to, 'Go in peace to where you belong with my blessings. May you find the light and those who love you and are waiting to greet you.' Repeat the blessing after scattering the salt.

◇ Sweep up the salt after twelve hours and tip it outside the house, repeating the words you said when you blessed each room against the paranormal presence.

✧ Finally, walk from room to room with your crystal sphere saying in the centre of each, 'Light, life and loveliness only remain in this place.'

✧ If the weather is good, open downstairs windows and external doors after using the salt water and leave them open for five minutes to let the energies of the natural world bring in fresh ch'i, or life force.

A GHOST CHILD

The idea of a ghost child is distressing as we would not like to imagine any child alone, without a mother or father. In fact, the majority of ghost children are merely apparitions, as the death of any child is so against nature it imprints on the aura of the place. This apparition is amplified and frozen in time by the grief of those around it. Mercifully, the memory preserved is usually of the happy child. If there was a huge tragedy of war or widespread disease, then a group of children may be heard or seen playing together. If you want to read about such cases, my book *The Psychic Power of Children* contains many examples.

Spirit children who do respond as presences are usually invisible friends or little spirit guardians. While they are usually attached to a child they may occasionally appear to an adult, and as a clairvoyant you will see them. If the child of the house is happy with this invisible friend you can reassure worried parents the presence is entirely benign and will fade as the child becomes involved in school and earthly companions. In the unlikely event you come across a true child presence who seems lost or sad, or a family reports frequently hearing distressed crying, you will see the ghost's deceased family hovering by, anxious to attract their attention. You need no candles or incense. Just hold the hand of the ghost child as you would a living child and show them the waiting family. Explain they are waiting to take care of them. The child will run towards them and when he or she reaches the spirit family they will fade, as will the light that you can detect surrounding them all.

FOLLOW-UP ACTIVITIES AND RESEARCH

✧ Book a walking ghost tour in an unfamiliar town. Before the walk, explore the area extensively, wearing thin-soled shoes. Either use a pendulum or tune in with your hands extended in front of you. Discover as much as you can about the presences and impressions you feel, hear and see. Of course, the area will be overlaid with hype and tourists, but even so there must have been strong paranormal presences to give rise to the tour in the first place. When you go on the actual tour, you can check known presences. If you saw or identified other ghosts check in the local library for a factual history of the area.

✧ Read a book about legends and ghost sightings near to your home and visit the haunted places to compare your feelings and insights with those you read.

✧ Begin your own book of sightings and hauntings, both in the local vicinity and whenever you go away. Check local records especially for major events and local personalities you may have identified.

✧ Find out the anniversary of a major battle or go to an ancient sacred site on one of the big spiritual festivals such as the Summer Solstice where people have visited the site on the same day for thousands of years. Try to identify ghosts from different periods and also features that no longer exist that you can verify on an old map.

✧ Plan your own method of dealing with difficult ghosts. Keep a dossier of cases and note what worked. If you do come across strong paranormal negativity, enlist the help of a really experienced medium rather than risking causing yourself distress.

✧ Join an overnight or weekend ghost watch at a haunted site and observe how it is organised. What worked, and what would you change if you were in charge?

TEN

Clairvoyance and Animal Communication

One of the fastest-growing areas of clairvoyance is pet therapy: dealing with animals' behavioural problems. You may choose to work just with your own animals and local wildlife, or to help pets and livestock of friends, colleagues and family. Indeed, one of the fastest ways to develop your own spiritual powers is to work with animals.

PET THERAPY: UNDERSTANDING AN ANIMAL'S ESSENTIAL PERSONALITY

Problems can occur if an owner misunderstands the basic personality of a pet. A small soft-eyed spaniel with the personality aura of a roaring lion needs to hunt his food (as much as possible) and to run free in an open space even if a city dog. In contrast, a huge stallion may have the temperament of a small shy pony and need protection from other horses or from being startled by roadworks.

Reading a pet's aura is a good first move. Interpreting animal auras is only slightly different from human auras and the colour meanings are the same. Indeed, by reading an owner's aura and seeing if the pet's aura mirrors it, you may see that the difficulties the animal is having are coming partly from the owner's stress. With practice you can do pet aura readings from photographs of the pet, even if emailed to you, but more easily if the owner is with you.

READING ANIMAL AURAS TO UNDERSTAND THE HIDDEN CAUSES OF PROBLEMS

In an animal aura there are three main bands of coloured light that extend progressively outwards from the creature's body. Animal auras are especially clear around the head, the paws, along the back and to a lesser extent round the stomach and heart. The more intelligent the pet, the more clearly defined the aura will be. Even in small animals like rabbits, guinea pigs and domestic birds you can detect this moving energy field.

If you are working with a specific animal, observe it in a variety of situations to get an overview of its aura changes: when resting, excited, hungry and being petted. But if you only get to see the animal briefly, make allowances for the circumstances. Check if the species aura described below is of the colour you would expect. Note the brightness and the width of the aura bands. Are any of the colours harsh, indicating hyperactivity, aggression or, in a female, about to come on heat? Are there any pale, faded or small aura bands which can indicate fearfulness, over-dependency on the owner or that the creature is being bullied by another animal, maybe a new pet in the household? Are there any very dark streaks or zigzags suggesting constant ongoing stress?

THE SPECIES AURA BAND

The species colour is common to all creatures of the same species and is closest to the body. This band of light closely follows the contours of the pet's body and is strong around not only the paws and head, but stomach as well as the back. The species aura may seem to be joined to the fur or feathers. This colour appears rippled, like a textured paint on a wall. It will vary in brightness and size according to the environment the pet is living in and its physical condition.

The more a pet becomes part of the family, especially if owned by one person who spends a lot of time with it, the more the personality and mood auras will dominate. These may mirror the moods and personality of the owner, which makes people say that pets and owners often look alike, but should not do excessively. Each aura band has a vital function in the pet's well-being. If the species aura is virtually non-existent, pale or dull, the pet may have lost its natural protective instincts and rely too closely on humans. This can result in an animal becoming neurotic, over-possessive of the owner, or eating too much as its natural appetite regulation is overridden by the association of food with approval.

You can advise a concerned pet owner that the pet with a deficient species aura may need more exercise and contact with nature. In the case of a domestic bird, more flying time and a companion may be helpful.

SPECIES AURA COLOURS

More intelligent and readily trained species of pets (dogs, horses, and birds such as parrots or parakeets that interact closely with humans) may have yellow in their species aura as well as the more usual green, pink or brown. Green is common around any domesticated animals kept as pets and indicates responsiveness to human affection and innate loyalty to their owner and family. It may be hidden in a traumatised animal under red or grey from the mood and personality bands.

The females of all species display a soft pink aura when they are pregnant, giving birth or caring for their young, and this remains among bitches, mares and ewes, even if they have given birth many years before. This will be mixed with a reddish glow even in gentle mothers as they protect their young against possible danger. Rabbits, guinea pigs and other small animals kept as pets may also have a pink rather than green aura, especially the females of the species.

Brown is a colour predominant among pets that spend many hours outdoors and close to nature, such as horses, donkeys and working dogs. However, some brown should be present in the species aura of all pets, even city ones. A total absence can indicate they are losing touch with their animal instincts. Grey is associated with shy pets, such as hamsters, gerbils, rodents, chipmunks, turtles and tortoises unless they are frequently petted to domesticate them.

THE PERSONALITY AURA

The personality colour band which forms the middle layer of the aura tends to be fairly consistent from the animal's early life, unless the pet is affected by serious abuse or neglect. As well as the head and paws, the personality colour is also strong around the heart and the pet's back, especially in the area that lies directly above the heart cavity in the chest. It affects the stomach area less. Its colour has quite a smooth matt texture, though when the pet is active, coloured lights may flow diagonally from it. In rescue animals the original personality aura can be retrieved from a misty or dark covering with patience and care. This is the area where dark stress streaks are most often visible.

The personality aura band is less defined than the innermost species aura.

THE MOOD AURA

The mood colour, the outermost and most volatile, is most easily affected by outside forces. Because of this changeability, it is the easiest and fastest to modify by small practical changes.

The mood is constantly moving with flashes and sparkles and becomes very active when the pet is excited or on the move. This band of the aura is seen most clearly around the head and the paws, claws or hooves as these pick up a great deal of information from the earth during a walk. The stomach is also affected by the mood aura and if the aura seems very harsh round the stomach area a light diet for a week or two may calm the pet.

An over-sensitive mood aura can make a dog very jumpy or make a cat hiss and scratch and a bird screech seemingly without cause. Animals may also become unduly afraid to be touched. You can recommend a calm environment with places to hide. There may be a boisterous person who hypes up the animal, or a child secretly teasing them. This can result in the pet urinating or defecating indoors as the bowels and bladder can be adversely affected by an overactive mood aura. Tune into the animal telepathically to find the cause if questioning the owner does not reveal the answer.

A good ongoing remedy is to soak a single piece of jade, rose quartz, amethyst or blue lace agate for a few hours in drinking water. Jade is especially good at calming neurosis, and amethyst works for obsessive behaviour. Remove the crystal and offer the water to the pet.

The mood aura follows the body least closely and merges with the air around and with the ground beneath the pet.

MODIFYING THE AURA

The best way to counteract over-brightness or harshness in any colours in the aura bands is the antidote colour. If an aura colour is pale you can suggest to the owner adding the same colour in a more vibrant shade. Apply the needed colour as a coloured collar, ribbon on a bridle, or crystals near where the animal sleeps.

Antidote colours:
  White: Green, brown or gold
  Red: Blue
  Orange: Indigo
  Yellow: Violet, purple
  Green: Orange (often needs no antidote)
  Blue: Red
  Purple: Yellow

Pink: Darker shades of blue
Brown: Green
Grey: Clear white
Black streaks: Any clear light colour, as white may be too intense

PET THERAPY FOR DEEP-SEATED TRAUMA

After the result of an aura reading, if conventional training methods and routine modification have not improved the animal after a week or two and it has been checked by a vet or qualified homeopathic animal physician, use the following method. You can do this with horses and other large animals.

✧ Establish whether the problem has always existed or if it has only recently occurred.

✧ If it's a recent problem or has suddenly become worse, ask the owner if there was an incident that upset the animal: an attack by another animal or jealousy towards a newcomer to the home.

✧ If there is no known cause, sit quietly by the animal and talk soothingly in a whisper as close to the animal's ear as it will allow you, all the while stroking it if it will let you. With a nervous or aggressive animal, sit where you can see the animal and stroke the pet telepathically by brushing the air at animal height and whispering aloud that the animal will soon feel better and you will help.

✧ You need to merge your aura with the pet's. Look through half-closed eyes towards the pet and think or whisper gentle loving words. Some pets, such as cats, do not like direct eye contact.

✧ Breathe gently as you focus on the pet's breathing pattern and link your mind to the rhythm of its heartbeat.

✧ Synchronise your breathing pattern with the animal's even if you cannot physically hear it. Imagine yourself as twin creatures moving slowly closer and closer. Imagine the twin outlines merge so that there is just one creature.

✧ Stop consciously imitating the breathing.

✧ Once you have merged your own aura with the pet aura you need to take a small step backwards in your mind, so that you are still within the joint aura, but at the same time can guide the experience. In this way you can see from the pet's perspective any deep-seated or immediate but hidden problem.

✧ You may feel sudden fear or anger as you see an image of the recent event that has caused the problem for the pet.

✧ Picture pink mist flowing through the joint aura, calming the fear and the painful image, gradually dissolving into tiny beams of pink light and floating away. Whisper in your mind you have taken away the distress and it will not return.

✧ If you now feel calm you may have solved the problem.

✧ However, sometimes you will feel the same fear or restlessness, though reduced in intensity. This would indicate that the problem has deeper roots. Remain within the animal aura. This time, imagine yourself as the animal until the fear intensifies. Hold your emotions steady even if you feel panicked. The animal will not be suffering as you are taking on the experience.

✧ You will now become aware of a scene when the animal was younger and the feelings of terror or confusion may become temporarily stronger.

✧ Relax and project a stronger pink light through the aura. As before, picture the scene breaking up into small pink light beams and leaving the animal, replaced by a sense of calm and maybe sleepiness.

✧ Then slowly reverse the process and gradually take back your own breathing.

✧ Whisper to the animal (either actually or telepathically) that the danger has passed and will never return because the owner will keep the animal safe.

MORE ADVANCED PET THERAPY

✧ If the troublesome behaviour persists even after treatment, or you are working with rescue animals, you may need to deal at an even deeper level with the trauma. Repeat the process until you reach the stage where you can see and feel the original traumatic event through the pet's eyes.

✧ Now you are going to try to superimpose a new happy ending over the distressing image, in which the pet was not hurt. Imagine the new scenario in as much detail as you can, picturing rays of golden light pushing the image round the pet's aura and the bad scene fading.

✧ Replay the scene as though on a screen in the pet's mind as you remain within its aura, as many times as necessary.

✧ If a trauma is really deep seated it will take a number of sessions and it will be painful for you as you relive the trauma time and again.

✧ After any trauma work it is important to sprinkle water over your higher chakras to cleanse your own energy field from the sorrow. Afterwards go into the open air to absorb the life force in nature.

BECOMING A PET DETECTIVE: FINDING LOST PETS

As well as using the following techniques to find any of your pets who go missing, you can help others to locate missing animals. The psychic tracking method depends on activating the invisible energy lines or tracks that exist between a person and their animal even when they are separated. These invisible lines are called psi lines by the Swedish energy researcher Göte Andersson (though not specifically in connection with animals). British biologist Dr Rupert Sheldrake described similar morphic fields: invisible connectors that link people and animals that are in close emotional contact and that remain in the background even when the creature and its owner are physically separated. Because these psychic links are two-way, it may be possible both to locate the missing pet and at the same time to psychically draw the pet home along the energy lines.

If the pet went missing after the owner moved house, it is possible to draw the animal to the new location through the emotional link between animal and owner. The method can also be used if a valuable animal, such as a pedigree breeding dog, horse or livestock animal, has been stolen and the police have not been able to make progress. You can use precisely the same methods for locating lost, mislaid or stolen items and, once you are very experienced, for trying to help locate missing people.

CREATING A PSI LINE CONNECTION

✧ If possible, go to the home and ask for a photograph. Facing the direction you instinctively feel the pet went (or the direction the owner advises you of), hold the photograph or, if you prefer, an item belonging to the pet, and picture the pet with the item.

✧ If in your home or consulting room, hold a photograph of the missing pet or a small item belonging to it and ask also for the person to bring a photo of the home. For a phone consultation, ask the owner to describe the pet in as much detail as possible, including anecdotes to link you with the essential creature, describe the home, and, if possible, email you a picture of the pet and home.

✧ Softly call the pet aloud three or four times (you could ask the owner, if present, to do this) and imagine a line of small lights leading from the pet's home into the distance.

✧ Try to visualise how far the lights are extending and the place where the trail ends. Does it seem to end relatively close to the house, a few miles or a long way distant? This will help the owner to direct the actual search or advertise to the correct area.

✧ Now activate the psi or morphic energies by saying the name of the pet aloud and also, 'Now you are safely home again. You can find the way.'

✧ Picture the pet at the end of the lights and now imagine it walking or flying, following the lights towards its home. Imagine an energy from the centre of your brow drawing the animal like a magnet.

✧ Now try to see the location at the end of the lights in case the pet is still too frightened or confused to respond. If you do feel fear keep sending soothing words via your mind.

✧ Slowly widen the image of the area round the pet very slowly and you may see something that distinguishes the place. If the pet seems trapped within a building, widen the image even further till you can see the exterior of that building. Extract as much detail as possible.

✧ Ask the owner if they can identify the place and, if not, refocus to try to obtain more identifying details.

✧ If the pet does not come within a day or two, repeat the process and refocus on the location; if it is the same one you saw before, the pet may have been taken in as a stray or by someone who wanted a dog or cat of their own and may not be allowing it outdoors.

✧ If the location is still not clear, or the search in the identified area unsuccessful, this is not a reflection on your ability but that the animal may be unwilling or unable to be found.

✧ Suggest the owner places a lamp in the window each night, and before bed calls the animals softly three or four times. If possible the lamp should be left on until daylight.

HOW DO YOU KNOW IF THE PET HAS GONE FOREVER?

✧ When you first tune in and call the pet you may have a sense of emptiness. It will feel as though someone has left a room. When you try to picture the pet you may just see mist. This does not mean that the pet has died, but that it is no longer connected to the owner.

✧ It is certainly worth persisting with the above methods to see if the link can be restored. It can be very hard to accept the pet is not coming back, but if the owner has made all possible practical attempts to find their animal, then it may be necessary to gently encourage the owner to let go with love, but to say the animal will always be welcome to return.

✧ If you can tune into the pet's new home clairvoyantly, you can tell the owner the area the pet is in and how it was rescued; it can be reassuring for an owner to know a beloved pet is being cared for. If the area is identifiable then the original owner may get a response if they advertise there and the new owner realises the animal is a stray.

✧ If the pet has died, the sensation is different: a lightness like a slight dizziness and a sense of peace but sadness (see Chapter Eleven).

HOW TO FIND A LOST ANIMAL USING A PENDULUM

✧ A pendulum can be used for tracking a missing pet that is in the vicinity of its former home or in the area where you detected the pet psychically.

◇ Begin by establishing a telepathic link with the lost pet as in the previous exercise. Hold the pendulum over the pet's bed or a photograph of the creature and picture it in your mind.

◇ Ask the owner to tell you about a happy memory concerning the pet.

◇ Attach a few pet hairs to the pendulum, if the owner has any from a grooming brush or the pet's bed.

◇ Holding the pendulum, close your eyes and you may receive a sudden vivid image in your mind that appears and fades very quickly.

◇ Call the image back by focusing on the pendulum. It will return more slowly, giving you time to tune in to where the animal may be.

◇ If not, at a boundary to the animal's usual territory or where it was last sighted, start walking straight ahead – the pendulum will swing positively – until the pendulum gives you the negative swing response. This indicates you have lost the trail.

◇ If you get a negative response immediately, stand on the spot and turn slowly in another direction till you get the positive movement.

◇ Start moving again. Call the animal softly to establish the psychic link and at some point you'll hopefully be heard.

◇ If the pendulum stops moving or becomes negative at any point, turn slowly and ask the pendulum if you are uncertain: 'Am I on the right track?'

◇ When you get very close to the pet, the pendulum will begin to vibrate and you may feel as if it is being pulled down by gravity. This may or may not replace the positive swing. This is because it is connecting with the animal's psychic energies.

✧ Stop at this point and call the animal's name loudly. Explore any outbuildings or deep hedgerows where the animal may be stuck. Ask owners of nearby properties if you can check their sheds and garages.

✧ Ask locally for sightings of a stray and put up notices round the immediate area.

Locating the Pet on a Map

✧ If the pet has been missing for some time and the pendulum fails to get a response in the immediate area, the pet may have moved further away. You can also use a map in your own home to help a client to pinpoint the location of the pet more specifically.

✧ Use a very detailed large-scale map of the immediate area. Ask the pendulum to indicate the location of the missing pet with a positive 'yes' response.

✧ Hold the pendulum over the top left corner of the map, move the pendulum slowly from left to right, top to bottom, over every grid square of the map until it begins to circle with a weak movement. Focus on that grid square and the movement will get stronger as it gets nearer to the pet.

✧ When it reaches the correct spot, the pendulum may also vibrate and seem to pull down.

✧ At this point put your other hand around the pendulum so you are not touching it but forming a cup round it. Close your eyes and tune into the pet in your mind using the vibrations of the pendulum as a psychic antenna.

✧ Use an even more detailed map of the grid square to pinpoint the location.

✧ If you get no response over the original map, try holding the pendulum over a map of an even wider area until you get a positive response.

Finding a Grid Reference using the Pendulum

✧ Another method, using a large-scale map, involves moving the pendulum along the bottom edge, left corner to right corner, and asking the pendulum to make a positive swing when it is in a straight vertical line with the animal's location. Draw a vertical line with a ruler to mark this.

✧ Then travel down the left hand side of the map from top to bottom and ask the pendulum to indicate with its positive swing when it is in a straight horizontal line to the pet. Draw a horizontal line across the map and where the two lines meet is the approximate location.

✧ With all these methods, the information is accurate at the time of the reading but the animal may move on so try to begin an actual search as soon as possible.

FOLLOW-UP ACTIVITIES AND RESEARCH

✧ Buy a highly illustrated wildlife or pet magazine and, with your eyes closed, open it any page and try to visualise as much as you can about the creatures and the setting. Then look at the picture and see how accurate you were.

✧ When someone mentions their pet, try to picture as much as you can about it and then ask if he or she has a photo or ask for more details to see if your psychic picture was accurate.

✧ Before going to a zoo, try to visualise two or three specific animals or birds from species you know are kept there and before the visit identify one out of the group that has distinguishing features. Check if you are right on the visit.

✧ When you visit a conservation area or zoo, if you cannot see a particular animal in its habitat, do not read the label on the fence but try to picture the hidden creature in detail.

✧ If you have time to observe, identify the area of undergrowth where you sense it is hiding and if you focus on it telepathically waking and coming out, it may emerge within a few minutes.

✧ If you are going to a house where you know there are pets, try to visualise them in advance and any details of the pet bed or toys in the bird cage. Be as precise as possible.

ANIMAL HEALING

✧ Begin a healing book in which you write the names of pets or animal species you wish to help. Put them in order of how urgently they need help.

✧ Ten p.m. is the traditional time for absent healing and if you have time dedicate one evening a week to your distance healing work. Wednesday, the day of Raphael, the healer archangel, is a good day for any kind of healing work.

✧ Light a white candle.

✧ Open the healing book at the first page and read aloud the name of the pet or species and what healing you seek.

✧ Ask the help of Hariel (the angel of pets), your own guardian angel or of St Francis, the patron saint of animals.

✧ Leave the book open at the page and pass your crystal pendulum in alternate anticlockwise and clockwise circles around the name while picturing rays of crystalline light flowing around and within the pet, or protection enclosing the endangered species.

✧ Choose one or two more names, according to the time you have, and work with the pendulum.

✧ Then read the names of any other pets listed and say, 'May they be healed/protected when and how best it shall be.'

✧ At this point either blow out the candle or, if you prefer, leave it burning in a safe place. If the pet cannot be made well the healing will ease the passing (see the next chapter).

ELEVEN

Mediumship

Mediumship, the ability to communicate on behalf of others with people who are no longer physically present on earth, is a natural gift that can be developed with practice and training. Anyone who has ever sensed the presence of a loved one at home, smelled their perfume or felt the fur of a former dog or cat brush against their leg, is manifesting spontaneous mediumship abilities. The practised medium, however, can tune easily and rapidly into the spirit world at the request of others.

Though some people do *see*, sense or dream about their deceased relatives or pets, and so feel the continuing affection, others are either blocked by grief or would not wish to make direct contact. In such cases a medium can offer a grieving person reassurance that a relative is happy in the afterlife. If a younger person has died, parents may need reassurance that they are being cared for by relatives in the afterlife and will continue to grow and thrive there. Alternatively, someone at a time of a major decision may seek advice from a deceased relative as they would have done in life, in the belief the relative may have extra information from the spirit world. Once more the medium can make the connection on behalf of the questioner.

ANIMAL GHOSTS

Usually when someone asks you about a deceased pet, or if you visit a house where an animal has recently died, you will see the animal close to the owner. Animals are quite solid phantoms and it is often only an ethereal light around them that offers the clue they are spirits. In essence, animal mediumship is no different from ordinary mediumship except you will not get messages from the animal.

FINDING A SPIRIT GUIDE FOR MEDIUMSHIP

You may already know your spirit guide, perhaps a deceased beloved grandmother, or a former mentor now in the afterlife who is with you in times of trouble or loneliness. As your clairvoyant gifts develop, wiser spirit teachers will move closer to you. You may by this stage in the course already be spontaneously encountering a wise Native North American guide or a similar evolved being from an ancient, spiritual culture. Your guide will either channel messages and information from the deceased relatives of those who consult you or, as many mediums prefer, remain protectively in the background as you communicate directly with spirits. Your guide can, if a spirit is having difficulty getting through to you, work with the guide of the person consulting you to strengthen the connection.

Whenever you call your guide before beginning any medial work, you will sense a tingling in your fingers and perhaps a warm gentle touch on your shoulder and a sense of being watched over lovingly. You may have experienced this sensation as a child and could sense a parent or grandparent standing behind you, even though you could not see or hear them. When you sense your guide with you, you can feel secure that any harmful paranormal influences will be filtered out, though psychic protection is still very important before working directly with the afterlife. There are no objective definitions of the afterlife, for we filter this unknown realm through the human mind.

DIFFERENT KINDS OF MEDIUMSHIP

The majority of professional mediums enter a light trance state during a private sitting or public demonstration and may also carry out healing work using their spirit guides. This kind of mediumship is what is called mental mediumship, where the medium receives information from the spirits via a spirit guide or directly through clairvoyant visions, clairaudience and clairsentience.

The messages from the spirit world are transmitted in words, generally using the medium's own voice. The medium can simultaneously communicate with the living person seeking the contact and the spirit world. The deceased person will hopefully offer idiosyncratic or personal information, so that the recipient can identify the spirit. The mental medium may *see* the spirit through clairvoyance or *hear* them through clairaudience and so identify an accent or unusual turn of phrase, but the sitter, unless clairvoyant, will not. If working in a deep trance, much less common in modern mediumship, a medium's voice may change into that of their guide. Physical mediumship most often takes place in this trance state. This is the medium's spirit guide or a spirit with prior permission temporarily taking over the body of the medium and transforming the medium's features into that of the deceased person. This requires a number of safeguards as it can be risky to be taken over even briefly and with a spirit guide acting as mediator. If you want to explore deep trance mediumship, I have suggested contacts on page 229 which will help you find out about more formal training.

CONNECTING WITH THE REALMS OF SPIRIT

If you are relatively new to mediumship there is no substitute for watching older and more experienced mediums at work, not necessarily just those with media attention, but those who do the rounds of spiritualist churches month after month, often for very little remuneration. If you wish to become a professional medium, at first sit in a regular open circle at a spiritualist church. Then begin to offer your services at small meetings or spiritualist churches to build up your skills and experience at dealing with different people – some of whom may be sceptical, fearful or even hostile and trying to catch you out.

BEGINNING MEDIUMSHIP IN EVERYDAY LIFE

✧ Begin with the spirit guides and deceased relatives of people that you see regularly in daily life whose family history isn't familiar to you. Look to the side or just behind a person as they talk to you and soften your eye focus so you are totally relaxed. A picture of the spirit guide may build up slowly and at first mistily, as when you see ghosts. However, there tends to be more vibrancy and colour as the spirit is emotionally linked to the person. This is always an actual presence. There may be more than one relative present or perhaps someone from an older culture or an ancestor in old-fashioned clothing.

✧ If you cannot see the face of the spirit clearly, close your eyes and their face will come clearly into your mind. Open your eyes again and focus more directly so you can see any distinguishing features the spirit has. An animal lover will be surrounded by creatures they have helped.

✧ The guide or relative may bring messages telepathically and you may hear their distinct voices, even accents, in your mind.

✧ Weave any information you gained into a casual conversation about where the living person's family come from or the professions their family practised generations back to verify your findings.

✧ You can then watch for spirit guides and deceased relatives on trains and buses, and when you meet anyone new. You will know instinctively by a strong warm feeling extending between your stomach and heart if you are making an actual connection, even though you cannot verify the information. Spirit guides who are not direct relatives tend to be slightly more ethereal and you will sense calm and harmony and more detached kindness, whereas a relative will exude love and warmth. You will soon instantly know the difference.

DEVELOPING YOUR MEDIAL POWERS

✧ Suggest to a sitter that they bring along an item belonging to the deceased person they want to contact (other relatives in the afterlife may come through as a result of the initial connection, or occasionally instead).

✧ Ask the sitter what they hope from the contact – whether to be reassured about the well-being of deceased family members in the afterlife or to ask for their advice about current worries.

✧ Welcome your spirit guide and wait to feel a tingling in your hands and aura.

✧ Ask the sitter to touch the item at the same time as you do to link you with the spirit's energy via the family connection and link of love.

✧ As you both touch the item, allow the energies of the sitter and the owner of the item to flow together. Ask the questioner to picture their deceased relative and recreate in their mind the loved one's voice telling a joke or expressing a catchphrase. Then take the item yourself between your hands and keep holding it.

✧ There may be issues troubling the questioner that they may wish to tell you about, for example if there was no chance to say goodbye, a lingering guilt about a stupid quarrel or coldness not mended in time just before the loved one died. Grief can make people forget all they did for a sick or elderly relative over months or years and dwell on the one unkind remark or impatience. In the modern world, the medium may have to act as counsellor and priest to relieve unnecessary but understandable regrets as well as trying to offer proof of survival of the relative after death.

✧ The advantage of private over a public demonstration of mediumship is that a session need not be based on receiving random messages from whatever spirits that draw close and then having to identify the correct recipients, but loving contact will be established directly between the deceased and the sitter with you as the intermediary.

✧ Wait and allow the impressions or images of the presence to build up. The deceased relative will usually stand close to the family member and the room may become noticeably colder as the presence manifests. You and the sitter may initially feel the hairs on your arms stand up, though this decreases as the affection between the two develops into a warmer feeling. This is not so with a spirit guide where the air remains cool. The sitter may become aware of the presence of the loved one without you saying anything and may become emotional.

✧ Just before the presence appears you may feel a slight vibration in your hands and feet and around your head as your own aura tunes into the spiritual energy of the spirit.

GUIDING THE SESSION

✧ If an entirely different spirit comes through there may be a good reason, so describe the spirit and the purposes for their visit may become clear.

✧ Do not keep stopping to ask if you are right or seek reassurance from the owner, as anxiety can block you and may break the flow. Focus on what you can see in your mind or externally rather than worrying if you are getting it wrong. Worrying is a guaranteed way to block yourself.

✧ Deceased relatives of a friend or client may show you symbols that have meaning for the person you are working with. Or they may convey an unusual phrase, recall an event they attended, an acquaintance they both knew or you may see actual pictures of shared moments with the sitter. You may see details of the face and clothing of the relative in your mind's eye.

✧ Describe what you are being shown as you receive it and when the flow ceases then ask your sitter if it means anything.

✧ When you can see no more, ask the sitter what they felt as you were talking when the spirit was present.

✧ Remember that the person who has asked you for a message may be in a vulnerable state and that you should try to put a positive spin on what the relative has said so the sitter feels that there is hope. Soften any warnings into advice on how to avoid possible hazards.

✧ Ask the sitter if they have anything they wish to say to the relative. Light a special candle to use as a focus. When they are ready they can blow out the candle and send the light to the relative. There may be a sign, a sudden fragrance, the candle smoke curling round the person or they may suddenly feel the relative, maybe for the first time. Usually this is followed by a dream or visit to the home by the spirit relative. What has been blocking communication will be cleared.

✧ A sitter may be curious about their spirit guide and you can show them using your clear crystal sphere, a dark mirror, or just allowing the image to build up in your mind and describing the guide. Give as much information as you can, including the reason the guide is not a relative, if this is the case. It could be because of the sitter's innate healing gifts, for example if the guide who has chosen them was skilled with herbs in their lifetime. Your client or the person you are helping informally may subsequently tell you that they are fascinated by herbs but were unsure about training as a healer.

✧ Afterwards thank all those guides and spirits who have manifested or offered information. End the session with the all-important, 'Return to your world in peace and with blessings or remain as friends and protectors. Blessings be on all both here and in the hereafter.'

✧ Extinguish any candles by blowing them out and send the light into the cosmos.

WHAT IF YOU DO NOT RECEIVE WHAT YOU HOPED FOR?

✧ If some of the information cannot be verified or the sitter says it is not accurate, do not panic as this may block your natural psychic flow. The owner may have forgotten the incident or your conscious mind may have intruded and interpreted the information as what seemed logical. Remember, however unlikely the picture you are receiving from the spirit, say exactly what comes to you, as it may have personal significance to the person you are working with.

✧ Check again with the spirit guide and if you feel a steady warm throbbing around your stomach and heart, trust yourself and say, 'This is what I am getting. So take it with you and it may make sense later.'

✧ If the presence does not manifest easily use the item as a link with the presence and you may extract enough information via the impressions, images and words you receive to reassure the sitter that the relative is well in the afterlife and to identify the spirit to the sitter.

✧ If something needs checking because it concerns family history, suggest the sitter discusses it with an elderly relative and in the meantime accepts the rest of the message if helpful.

✧ If you get only one piece of clear information say so, as that may be all that will come through. Even the best mediums may find themselves blocked, perhaps because of the grief or fear of the sitter. The sitter may be unconsciously preventing the desired spirits from coming through.

✧ I have seen even well-known mediums struggling to fill a session. Second-guessing is counterproductive and reduces the value of what was psychically received.

✧ Be honest and explain before the sitting that there is not a constantly open line to the afterlife, but that the strength of the reception can vary.

✧ Suggest the sitter puts the treasured item by their bed and holds it before sleep for a few days. The relative may appear in a dream with further advice. Then the sitter can, if wished, check back with you and you may find the link clearer.

✧ You could offer divination to give extra input to the question that prompted the visit.

✧ Finally, it may be that the deceased person was very private and would never have talked through a third party. In this case work to make the personal connection by teaching the sitter simple psychometry techniques and putting the deceased person's fragrance on the pillow to evoke the presence in dreams.

TELEPHONE AND EMAIL MEDIUMSHIP

Telephone and email mediumship offers opportunities for working with photographs of pets, people that have died and of their current families and homes to build up a psychic connection. Begin with direct voice contact through a pre-arranged phone consultation, especially if you already have photos emailed over to you. Hold the pictures in one hand and, closing your eyes, clasp the receiver to make the psychic circuit. Ask the person phoning to hold identical pictures in one hand and with the phone in the other. Keep talking and when you have finished discuss the findings.

If there are a number of questions to be considered, working via the Internet can be very successful. In email mediumship it will give you aura connections to work with that you can sense both with the living and with the deceased. If you have a picture of the two together have this by your computer and touch it with the hand you do not write with and type one-handed. Type without pausing. You can afterwards add other methods of divination or tune in by looking into your crystal ball to span the dimensions and *see* the deceased relative or the questioner's spirit guides, using the crystal doorway method. Having studied them put any pictures under the ball.

CALLING A PRESENCE OR SPIRIT GUIDE USING CANDLES AND DARK MIRRORS

Dark mirrors are natural gateways into other worlds and what you see may appear like a grainy black and white photograph or like an old-fashioned silent film where the images flicker intensely. Your dark mirror should, if possible, be made of darkened smoky glass. These will look almost opaque till candlelight shines in them. A dark mirror of A4 size is ideal.

Best of all are obsidian mirrors, though these are quite expensive, unless you choose a small one, but are fabulous for serious scryers. However, you can buy mirrors made from the same material as shiny black wall tiles or buy a large domestic black wall tile and frame it. A good substitute is a large, very thin slice of agate in purple or blue. Hold it up to any light source and if you can see your face dimly in it, then it is suitable.

SEEING WITHIN THE DARK MIRROR

Traditionally, dark mirrors are believed to provide a temporary home for an evolved guardian spirit. You can discover the spirit guide who will assist your mediumship by looking into the mirror. If after a few months a new guide appears then this is because you are developing your mediumistic gifts in new directions, perhaps healing others.

✧ Hang your dark mirror on a wall or prop it on a table away from windows or doors that might illuminate it. Dark scrying is best done in darkness except for candlelight. Draw the curtains if necessary.

✧ Have a flat surface in front of your dark mirror and position small candles along the base.

✧ Stand or sit so you can faintly see your own face within the mirror. By seeing yourself in the mirror you are setting your spiritual inner self at the threshold of other dimensions.

✧ Light the candles, polish the mirror with a cloth you keep for the purpose, ask for the protection of the four archangels and imagine them standing around you and the mirror in a protective square.

✧ Light protective incense such as rose, myrrh or lavender so the reflection of the smoke swirls in the glass.

✧ If you wish, hold a protective crystal such as smoky quartz, rutilated quartz, or amethyst.

✧ You can specify who you wish to contact in the mirror: your guide, who will assist your mediumship; a wise ancestor; a spirit teacher or healer guide of your own or the sitter; or a deceased relative.

✧ Open your eyes slowly and you will see in the mirror behind your face the spirit image of the chosen protector and feel the gentle loving shadowy presence standing behind you. Do not turn round. If you cannot see the image, close your eyes, open them again and blink, then look into the mirror.

✧ Try this for a third time and if it still does not work close your eyes still facing the mirror and let the light beams convey the form of the spirit into your mind.

✧ Ask if the guardian has a message for you and words will flow into your mind, spoken in the voice of the guide or ancestor, or you may hear them externally.

✧ When you are ready, thank the guardian and say, 'Go in peace and in blessings until we meet again.'

✧ Close your eyes and when you open them do not look into the glass but blow out the candles one by one and sit enjoying the fragrance.

✧ In the unlikely event you ever feel afraid while using a dark mirror, or find it hard to break the connection even with your loving guardian, say 'Blessings be', blow out the candles and then say 'Go in peace. I remain myself and separate. So shall it be.'

HELPING OTHERS WITH DARK MIRRORS

✧ This works well when helping others to find their spirit guides or to help you connect with their deceased relatives if the connection is only partial by other means.

✧ Hold the mirror up to the light of a single candle, but this time do not look directly into the mirror.

✧ Turn the mirror to create a circle of light using the candle reflection to act as a doorway. Ask to see the spirit guide or the relative of the sitter in the afterlife. Use their name if known.

✧ Keep looking at the point of light until the door opens. You may see the sitter's relative, tinged with light, perhaps in a happy scene enjoying a life similar to the best parts of their earthly one. This information can help to make death seem less daunting to the sitter.

✧ You will see their spirit guides in the same way if you request this aloud. If you are working with someone who is quite experienced they themselves can look in the mirror towards the circle of light and may see or sense the same scene and figure but in more detail. If they do not want to do this continue to look and describe what you see. You can also develop the sitter's visions by taking the mirror after they've finished, focusing again on the circle of light, expanding the images and also receiving messages from their guide or loved one.

AN ALTERNATIVE TO A SÉANCE

The dark mirror is a safer alternative to a séance where spirits who are present in the room are asked to make themselves known either telepathically or by using a ouija board and glass to spell out the messages. Low-life spirits tend to lurk round séances, especially ones using ouija letter boards, and can be very clever at imitating famous people from the past. Like many experienced psychic people, I spend a great deal of time trying to help people who have terrified themselves calling up spirits in a ouija session and subsequently cannot get rid of the spirit. More and more teenagers are calling up spirits, sometimes with dire psychological results. If you are very experienced and trained in mediumship you could lead a séance calling unknown spirits, as you can impose safeguards and be alert for any sitters getting frightened. I respect any medium who does hold responsible séances but I personally do not. If you read my book *Psychic Suburbia*, I have described cases where even mediums with years of practice have occasionally encountered problems with vicious spirits intent on possession of vulnerable people.

A DARK MIRROR GROUP SÉANCE

In an experienced psychic group, including some mediums, call the four archangels to cast a circle of light and pass the dark mirror around the group. The group should sit round a candlelit table and each look into the mirror slowly and ask to be shown a wise guide, a spiritual ancestor or a beloved relative who is close and to receive a message from them. The person holding the mirror should describe the vision they see and the others tune in by picturing the candlelit mirror in their minds. A great deal of unknown information can be received by the whole group that is verified in the days after the session.

Nasty spirits will rarely pretend to be spirit guides. If a guide is not known to the person, the group should check their authenticity by tuning into their stomach-to-heart area and you will feel if the energy is good. Each person receives a guide, ancestor or relative through the mirror and then these wise ones are welcomed into the circle of light. It is possible to detect the shimmering light presences forming a circle behind the sitters and often a collective vision is received of spirit realms. This is confirmed by the various group members. Then blow out the candles, sending the light to those who need healing, and sit quietly in the darkness till the glow of the spirit guides and ancestors fades. Thank the archangels and guides until you meet again. Light a single white candle and discuss the experiences of the group.

FOLLOW-UP ACTIVITIES AND RESEARCH

✧ Research the history of mediumship and spiritualism from 1848, when the Fox sisters, fourteen-year-old Margaret (Maggie) and Catherine (Kate), aged twelve, managed to communicate with the spirit of the peddler, Charles B. Rosa, who claimed to have been murdered years before in their house in Hydesville, near Rochester, New York State. In doing so they introduced the concept that it was possible to talk with the dead and receive information from them.

✧ Put together a simple teaching programme of ways sitters can make direct connections with a deceased relative or animal either during the session or at home afterwards, using crystals, fragrances and psychometry to induce the presence in dreams or by signs. This can be valuable to supplement information during a consultation, especially if an issue is ongoing.

✧ Go along to an evening of mediumship at a spiritualist church or local theatre and study how the medium works, whether they receive information, and then ask if anyone can identify the spirit, or go to various members of the congregation and describe a relative or animal standing close to the chosen people. Note how specific the information is or if it could apply to a number of people. Tune clairvoyantly into what the medium is seeing and see if you can obtain any additional information. If there is a chance afterwards talk to the medium or to the president of the spiritualist church about how they learned their art. Most are delighted to talk to an interested newcomer and if you meet the president you may get an invitation along to a circle evening.

TWELVE

Clairvoyancy as a Profession

For most people who develop clairvoyant powers it is virtually impossible to keep your gifts to yourself. Before long you will regularly be doing informal readings for colleagues, friends and families, finding lost pets and missing items, telling people about their past lives or helping them to make contact with deceased relatives.

As the months pass and your gifts grow, friends of friends will ask you for advice. For some people this informal way of using spiritual powers is very fulfilling, though it is important to set a limit to the time and energy you give to others. Value your gifts and others will value them also. Set limits so that people do not ring you at all hours of the day and night with their problems or expect you to stay after a long day at work without notice to do a reading whenever a love or family crisis arises. Even with informal readings it is important to fix times to suit you and to learn to say no.

WORKING FROM HOME AND HOW TO FIND CLIENTS AND PREMISES IF YOU DO NOT WORK FROM HOME

As you discover that you are becoming more and more accurate, it is perfectly possible to turn your clairvoyant abilities into a part-time or even full-time career. Clairvoyance is a perfect occupation to fit around school hours, if you are at home with children, or practise on the occasional evening or weekend as you begin to build up a client base. The advantage of working from home is that you can dictate your own hours and vary these according to other needs in your life.

Begin in a small way. You can also offer your services as a mobile clairvoyant if you have a car. Psychic coffee mornings or evenings, where one person invites a group of friends or family to their home and you read for each in turn, are a good source of income. For a single client, work on an hour minimum booking and charge modest travelling expenses to make it worthwhile.

EXPANDING YOUR BUSINESS

As your business expands it may be easier to rent a room in a central location that makes travel easier for clients as well as on-the-day drop-in customers – necessary while you are building your repu-tation. Choose a day such as market day when the area will be especially busy. Best of all is a New Age store that often has a read-ings area or room above the shop and attracts the kind of clients who are tuned into the idea of readings. If possible rent by the hour or, if you book for a day, try to get a reasonably full schedule by having an appointment list in the shop some weeks ahead. Ask if you can put a board outside to attract passing customers if you have any slots unfilled. Negotiate to pay between 20 and 25 per cent of your total takings to the store. The percentage method is a great incentive for a shop to fill your schedule.

Alternative health centres, holiday complexes or hotels in tourist areas may have rooms for hire. In the high season they may welcome a monthly lecture or demonstration for an hour in the evening, followed by the chance for you to do paid readings. As you become better known you can increase your prices. On Halloween and New Year's Eve there are always many parties so hotels and holiday complexes may welcome a resident clairvoyant. Contact them well in advance with ideas for a themed evening. Once you have established yourself, offer a ghost investigation, clairvoyance or mediumship weekend where you can combine demonstrations with teaching, such as how to read the tarot.

HAVE CRYSTAL BALL, WILL TRAVEL

If you are already experienced, you can use your gifts to travel. The Mediterranean has a huge English-speaking expatriate community, and spiritual centres are mushrooming from France to Greece and as far as Malta, as are psychic fair events. Since many of the population are retired there is a stable client base as well as holidaymakers. Renting an apartment, especially in winter when it is cheap, gives you not only a sunshine holiday but a chance to earn extra money. Usually the opportunities are greater at resorts than at recognised spiritual areas such as Sedona in Arizona, or Glastonbury in Somerset, where competition is fierce and rooms expensive to hire. In Australia there are as many astrologers as there are psychologists and there are increasing numbers of spiritual and clairvoyant lectures and workshops in every state.

Once you are well known in the media, it is possible to get work on cruise liners as a guest speaker, with the opportunity for private readings. At first, apply to modest mid-priced cruise lines with your CV, dates you are free a year ahead (though someone might drop out earlier through illness) and your specialities you could teach or lecture on. Even if a cruise is not very exciting or the ship not luxurious, get experience and then you can apply to more upmarket companies. Cruising is a good way to avoid winter weather and live comfortably.

THE PSYCHIC FAIR CIRCUIT

You need a good deal of stamina if you are going on to the psychic fair circuit, as you may have to work from around ten a.m. till six or seven p.m., two or three days in a row, with one reading after another. You may have to travel long distances carrying posters and heavy crystals. Psychic fairs vary from a few tables of clairvoyant readers and ten to fifteen stalls selling crystals and books at a one-day event, to a venue where there are over a hundred stalls and an organised programme of lectures, workshops and demonstrations, lasting between three days and a week.

Anyone can book a table at a psychic fair. Search for Mind, Body and Spirit festivals on the Internet to find a list of events in your location. You will have to book several months ahead with a deposit to secure your table at a popular festival. At smaller events, organisers welcome the offer of lectures and workshops though they may take part of the ticket money. At larger fairs and festivals you may be expected to give a free lecture as a chance to promote your own skills. Larger and more prestigious events will have more expensive tables, but since they are normally in the centre of major cities you can charge more for readings to offset the expenses. With more prestigious events, lecture spots are by invitation only so you need to send a CV detailing previous experience six months or more in advance. You will not make a fortune in fees even if your name headlines a festival, and as a subsidiary speaker you may not get much more than basic expenses. It can be better to settle for a free or reduced-price stall to do readings. You could approach a local hotel to organise your own event with a few friends and split the cost of the venue.

Often there is a team of established readers at hotel events who may move round different hotels. To get experience, offer yourself as a relief reader when someone is ill or on holiday. Remember, however, that, as the middleman, the organiser will take more of the profits. Many festivals and fairs are held at several different venues around the country throughout the year. These tend to have a core of mediums and clairvoyants who can initially be hard to get to know. However, do persist in making friends when they socialise after the show as you will learn a great deal about the best venues for fairs in the area, which events to avoid because they are poorly attended, and addresses of good but reasonably priced accommodation.

Try to offer one or two unusual psychic arts (such as sand reading in a small tray, Celtic tree staves, divination with a set of small crystals or perhaps past lives with a crystal ball) so that you stand out among the other readers. Usually you have a stall the size of a large card table so plan in advance how you will arrange it and take a beautiful tablecloth. Smudge round your table and tools before the fair and keep a bottle of mineral water to splash your brow and inner wrist points between readings. Smile and say hello to everyone that passes and engage in some small talk and offer your business card to anyone who stops. At the end of the day smudge again yourself, your tools and the table.

LECTURES AND MEDIUMSHIP DEMONSTRATIONS

Much of this activity will arise initially from psychic fairs or in conjunction with local spiritual centres. Lecturing itself tends not to be very lucrative unless you are very high profile. You may get half the door money or a set fee and expenses if you are lecturing for an established centre. However, it is a useful way of distributing your business cards and leaflets among an audience who are receptive to the New Age, especially if you offer telephone or email readings.

If you organise your own lectures you need to find a suitable venue in a central location and outlets, such as a local New Age store, who will sell advance tickets in return for a small cut of the profits or maybe space to sell their products at the venue. The venue itself may sell tickets. Once you are experienced, demonstrations of mediumship where you channel messages for members of the audience are always popular. Start with small venues if you are not experienced and limit numbers. In time you may be able to organise a monthly demonstration. Offer occasional alternatives to straight mediumship, especially with smaller numbers, to attract regular attendees. If you work well with psychometry, ask everyone to bring a flower of a kind they love or which reminds them of a deceased relative. These are put in a basket and you pick individual flowers and channel a message for the person who brought the flower. Have different coloured ribbons for people to tie round flowers if there is one the same already in the basket. Alternatively, for larger numbers have a spirit guide evening when you connect chosen individuals with their spirit guides and pass on any messages.

ORGANISING WORKSHOPS

Evening, half day or weekend workshops tend to be more lucrative than lectures. Larger New Age stores or spiritual centres may have workshop rooms ready equipped to rent. They generally provide advertising, take bookings, get the room ready, and may lend crystals or equipment from the shop. For this you may pay between 35 and 50 per cent of the total you make, especially if the centre is prestigious, very busy and based in a city centre with good transport links. Again, go for the percentage payment rather than flat rent in case a workshop is poorly attended or does not take place because of lack of numbers.

You need to pick popular subjects, not obscure ones which attract only a minority, but offer occasional unusual topics within the subject so your course stands out from the majority. You could plan a graded course over several weeks, for example in clairvoyance, with a test and certificate of attendance for those who complete the course. You could also offer an evening course in reading the tarot or psychic development. A further education college will pay you to run the course. They will advertise and book in the students. They will be planning new courses for September as early as the previous April so get your proposals in early.

TELEPHONE CLAIRVOYANCE

The advantage to telephone and online connections is that you can attract clients from other geographically distant events you attend, via your website. Phone readings are not very different from face-to-face consultations as the voice is a powerful transmitter of psychic energies. You need to chat initially for four or five minutes to make a strong link. Explain the methods you will be using, how you will work and find out what the person wants to know. You can comfortably build this into a session of half an hour or an hour.

You can ask the questioner to select cards, runes, crystals or staves. You should turn them over one by one or touch in turn a circle of face-down runes or staves and tell the person to stay 'Stop' or 'Now' whenever they feel a card or rune is for them. You can return the card or rune after reading to the pack or circle as if it is picked again you know it is of significance. As the reading progresses, describe the cards, runes or crystals you pick, or images you see in a crystal, and their meanings so the client can picture them and understand the reading. Check at every stage they are following the reading and encourage dialogue. Five minutes before the end ask if there are any other questions so you can bring the reading to a close. As for payment, unless it is a regular client who always pays on time, ask for money in advance; it is easy to set up a merchant account through an Internet banking site, such as PayPal. Get the client to phone you but rent an extra number on your landline and keep it just for for phone consultations.

PHONE LINE WORK

If you decide to work for an existing phone line choose one where the individual clairvoyants are advertised by name and with details on the net so people know about you and can choose you specifically. The calls are routed through a centre that takes credit card payments from clients, often for a set time with the option of buying more. These are more satisfactory than those where there is a big automated organisation and you are just one of numerous anonymous clairvoyants under pressure to keep the clients talking as long as possible. With these especially you need to check out the organisation to ensure you get paid regularly on time. You may be asked to undertake a phone test but you should ask that the questions are genuine and of meaning to the questioner. If you feel uncomfortable with the method of questioning or have negative feedback the organisation is not for you. You will see no more than around a third of the amount charged for the call, maybe much less. It can be suitable work if you are housebound for whatever reason, but difficult with small children as you are expected to do your set hours without any interruption. Also, with the less personalised lines, you have people constantly checking you and pressurising you to maintain longer calls.

CYBER CLAIRVOYANCE: HOW TO SET UP A PROFITABLE CLAIRVOYANT BUSINESS ON THE INTERNET

A website will advertise yourself and your services, both for online readings and other services such as psychic evenings or online courses. Researchers on shows and journalists writing articles often trawl the net for experts so if you can add some pages of research into topics you are interested in, then you will get far more visitors to your site. Keep your pages regularly updated, maybe adding a new topic every month, and you will get higher hit rates through the search engines and many returning visitors. It is possible for even a relatively inexperienced computer user to use website-designing software, but getting a professional to design your site is not prohibitively expensive. A student proficient in computers or a professional freelance web designer can provide a one-off layout and then, if you wish, maintain it for you.

You can, of course, offer email readings without having a website by just having your email address on business cards and any advertising. In this case use another email address from your main one as you may get a lot of unrelated enquiries. However, having a website, even a simple one, will more than double your business. On a website you can have an online form with the kind of readings you offer with prices for each. Ask the person to send you their list of questions, date of birth and that of any other person concerned in the questions and, if appropriate, photographs. You can scale your charges according to the number of questions, the nature of the reading and the methods used. Some people want a life review or past lives, others an answer to a straightforward question. Set a realistic timeframe for answering email readings and state this. If there is going to be a delay, let the client know in advance. Check for any bookings where there is an urgent, time-specific question and prioritise that email.

With a first-time client paying by cheque through the post, wait for the cheque to clear through the bank before carrying out the reading.

CORPORATE EVENTS

Going along by arrangement to a company's office party or doing short consultations for individual members of staff, perhaps at a company weekend training event, can be very lucrative. Such work is not easy to get and you have to present a very businesslike approach and appearance to be accepted. You will need professional looking publicity material and an application letter to send to the Human Resources offices.

When interviewed, emphasise how important it is for people to trust their intuition and how you can help people to make decisions rather than focusing on the more mystical angles (you may be asked to organise a training session on intuitive decision-making as a result). Ask in advance before each booking what is expected.

This might be serious individual consultations for stressed staff, in which case wear a city suit and take your tarot, etc. in a smart case, or a light-hearted social evening where you do instant readings for a large number of people, perhaps walking round with a basket of cards inviting people to ask a question and choose one or two cards for you to interpret. Take along business cards even to a fun evening and you may attract clients for private consultations. Claim a large flat fee plus travel and hotel expenses, if applicable.

WORKING WITH THE MEDIA: PITFALLS AND BENEFITS

The benefits of becoming established on the media circuit are huge as publishers, magazine editors and the general public value television appearances highly. Unless you are a resident expert on a programme, your fees in whatever country you work are unlikely to be very high and in many cases will be expenses only. But the prestige and publicity are worthwhile and will do wonders for your private bookings and your work in workshops and on the festival circuit.

There are pitfalls. Some programmes, especially investigative ones, unless live can be edited and some are slanted to test clairvoyants and mediums in ways they are almost bound to fail no matter how gifted they are. Be wary and ask questions about what you will be required to do. Unless you are very sure of the format and the integrity of the programme, avoid being tested for the benefit of the camera rather than the client. I have witnessed less gifted mediums hyped up because their face and personality fits a media ideal, while equally good genuine but less worldly clairvoyants and mediums can be made to look foolish. With discussion programmes, there is no use taking part if you have no chance of putting across a reasoned opinion or you have to shout above a baying crowd to be heard. Often extreme points of view are favoured over balanced ones as being better entertainment. Opt instead for even brief one-to-one interviews on shows with presenters whose work you trust, or a cameo in a quality documentary. Watch similar programmes before you go on a show to understand the format and how you will be treated.

ADVERTISING

In the modern world of high technology, it has never been easier to advertise. You need business cards to take everywhere and give to everyone you meet, whether clients or contacts at a fair or in the media. These should contain your name, a brief description of what you offer and a website or email address and phone number. Your hairdresser and any beauty salons or sports clubs you belong to are fruitful locations to leave cards, as are any crystal or New Age stores (you can offer a discount for people coming through these sources). You can design and print cards yourself if you are computer literate or buy cheap cards online. In either case, if you can personalise them with an attractive logo or your photograph they are more likely to be memorable.

Leaflets can be useful if you intend to offer a range of services such as psychic evenings, hen parties (a growing market) and psychic courses as well as your corporate services. These can easily be produced on a computer and can be distributed at events. Business can come through the most unlikely sources. For psychic fairs you need one or two easily transportable glossy posters or placards to put behind your stall with what you offer and prices and an all-important A4 advanced booking form with marked gaps for short breaks, for each day of any festival. Put this form, divided into appropriate time slots, on your table so people can sign their desired slots and not interrupt you during readings.

PUBLICITY SOURCES

When you start out you can advertise very cheaply in local free papers to bring in business. Local weekly, rather than daily, newspapers also tend to be intensively read. Look in New Age stores as there are often Mind, Body, Spirit magazines covering different regions that will advertise you cheaply. When you have more free money you could advertise in national New Age magazines as the take-up rate tends to be high for email or phone readings. In any source of publicity create a short, eye-catching advertisement that makes you stand out from other clairvoyants on the page. If possible, offer an added extra (such as a free astro prediction using a computerised method as your basis) when clients purchase a more extensive reading.

SAFETY ISSUES FOR CLAIRVOYANTS WORKING FROM HOME

⬥ If clients are known well to you then there is no problem seeing them at home. But inviting strangers you may only have spoken to on the phone is inadvisable unless you have someone else in the home when they call. Even then you need to be careful about locking away valuables, bank account details and cash, and not giving them free access to study entry points and your private possessions. Ninety-nine per cent of clients are perfectly honest, but it only takes one who is not to threaten your security or maybe return to steal your valuables.

⬥ Once someone knows your number and address, they can call any time, and if a client is vulnerable or emotionally unstable they may turn up at your home uninvited.

⬥ You could suggest a full phone consultation first or arrange to meet clients you are unsure about at a New Age store, and only if you feel instinctively secure give them a home contact. Trust your intuition, but also have earthly safeguards.

⬥ Equally, if you visit a client's home, whether for a private visit or a group evening, try to ascertain the person is who they say they are, arrange to be driven and collected first time to the door and ask the driver to wait while you go in and then phone them after five minutes to let them know it is OK.

✧ Even if you know a client, if an address they give is unfamiliar or you feel at all uneasy, always tell someone precisely where you are going, leave contact phone numbers and the time you will return.

FOLLOW-UP ACTIVITIES AND RESEARCH

✧ Draw up a business plan either for a new business or to expand an existing one. Find out about local and national grants for new businesses and about the business facilities offered by various banks, as these can vary greatly. New enterprise is welcomed in most regions and you may find all kinds of concessions and interest-free loans available to launch you during the early years that many people do not claim. A local Chamber of Commerce or Citizen's Advice Bureau is usually the best starting place.

✧ Work out the minimum income you will need to gradually make clairvoyance your main or only occupation. If you are new to professional clairvoyance this could take two or three years, so be patient and only give up the day job when you are showing a profit. However, you may be able to reduce to part-time working much earlier. You may be lucky and hit the big time rapidly but the majority of clairvoyants, even media ones, make a good but not spectacular living.

Testing Your Clairvoyant Skills

The greatest proof you have of your evolving clairvoyant gifts is in the positive feedback you get from readings as well as your own increased intuitive powers that influence aspects of your daily world for the better. However, I have suggested tests should you wish to assess your progress. Choose one, or attempt all the different levels of tests now and again to monitor your ongoing progress. In time you will be creating tests of your own should you need them and perhaps assessing your own students.

TEST 1: BASIC LEVEL

⟡ Repeat all of the exercise on pages 17–19 in Chapter One. Your overall success should be far greater than when you tried the different techniques at the beginning of the book and in an intermediary stage. You may now have strengthened your skills in those areas you found challenging.

⟡ If there are any areas where you still experience difficulties, analyse in detail why and adapt material in this book to create another approach to the subject. For example, if you find still-water scrying hard choose a day when the wind is rippling the water, where clouds and perhaps nearby trees are reflected within it so you have different shapes of light and darkness within the water to make actual shapes from which your psyche can extract psychic information. Once you are comfortable working with reflected images, gradually reduce the stimuli until you can expand a single point of light, whether outdoors or indoors with a candlelit bowl of clear water.

✧ Remember, even the best clairvoyants have areas of weakness and after you have read more books or attended or taken online courses on the problematic subject, combine the problematic method with one you are very gifted in. In this way the weak area will slowly evolve so if you took the test again in three or six months time, you would sail through.

TEST 2: CLAIRVOYANCE IN THE EVERYDAY WORLD

These exercises are marginally easier since you can draw upon the energies of nature or an old place to guide you. You may need to carry out the individual tests on different occasions, as some are time consuming and involve preparation. Some clairvoyants find these more meaningful than the abstract games in Test 3.

Work with a friend or family member and ask them to catch a bus or drive somewhere fifteen minutes from your home to as unusual a setting as possible. Ask them to phone you when they arrive, but just to identify themselves. Then switch off your phone. Allow an image of where the person is to come into your mind, following the psi line activated by the voice and using remote viewing. Expand your vision of the scene and note any distinguishing features. Write or draw every detail possible, note sounds, images, smells and feelings and sketch a map of the salient features of the location.

Ask the subject to stand in the place for five minutes after phoning and then to take a digital camera image or instant photograph and return it to you. Study the image and assess how accurate you were and where an apparently inaccurate feature may have some connection. For example a fountain you perceived that was not there was in fact someone watering flowers.

Set seven plants of approximately the same height and size in a row on a table: a single large cut flower in a vase without water, a flowering plant, a green ornamental plant, a growing herb in a pot, a cactus, an unhealthy plant and a plastic plant. Hold your palm chakras a few inches away from each plant and feel the difference in aura energies. Now get a friend or family member to blindfold you. They will rearrange the plants and gently guide your hands so they are as close as possible, but sufficiently high above each plant in turn so you cannot detect any physical difference.

Take your time and identify each plant from its aura and tune into its essential energies. Ask the person helping you to record the results. Two correct identifications is down to chance but more than that is a sign of evolved psychic power.

Visit an old house or castle that has been in the same family for at least two hundred years with a relatively unbroken history. You should not know anything about the place prior to the visit. Focus on a painting or, if there isn't one, a detailed description from a guide book of the founding ancestor. Next, find a photograph or painting of the present owner or the most recent family member to own the house.

Go outdoors or to a quiet area in the house. Picture as many details as you can recall of the two known members and imagine a line of light like a psi line between the two extending through the mists. Begin with the original owner furthest back in history and imagine him or her surrounded by family and then the succession or a new owner. Historically, castles and big houses suddenly changed owners if there was a war or the family fell out of favour with the monarch, so be alert for major energy shifts.

Visualise each owner as you see, hear and sense them, handing a key forward through the subsequent generations. *See* as though before you there is a procession of each new owner and immediate members of the family and any sudden early deaths or disasters. Write down in note form all you see, sense and hear in words about the time line, including any national or local events that affected the family, such as the Civil War in America or the First World War in Europe.

When you feel the connection fading, verify how much information was accurate or nearly accurate. Compare your notes with the actual history of the area in a local museum or archive or contact a local historian or archivist online if there are details that do not match but you are convinced are valid. If you see any of the family ghosts during your tour that is a bonus. Return to the spot you saw them and try to communicate.

Turn off the caller display on your mobile phone and aim to monitor the next ten phone calls. As the phone rings, picture either the person calling if you sense you know them, or allow an image of an unknown man or woman dialling the number and the reason for the call. If the caller is someone you know, picture what they are wearing and what they were doing just before the phone call and weave that into the conversation.

Repeat the exercise at least twice weekly until you have a hundred calls and see if you score above the significant mark, that indicates something clairvoyant is happening (see table in Test 3) and how far above that mark you score.

Try to psychokinetically and telepathically influence someone to call you. Choose a time when you will not be disturbed and pick someone for whom it may not be easy but is able to phone you at the time of the experiment. Initially strengthen the link by psychically calling the person. Either focus on a photograph or imagine them in your mind and say, 'Phone me now.' Say it louder and louder in your mind for a minute, then stop for a while and start again, then break again and restart so you call in your mind three times altogether.

If nothing has happened try again after an hour. Leave it and try again after three hours. If this doesn't work, try again the next day or the next convenient time with the same person. Of course this partly depends on how psychically receptive the other person is but you should aim to succeed within seventy-two hours if you work on consecutive days. The faster you make contact the more instantly activated your psychokinetic powers are.

TEST 3: MORE FORMAL TECHNIQUES

Even gifted clairvoyants can perform poorly at formal tests as the situation is inevitably artificial and not linked with emotional connections that are natural channels for transmitting psychic powers. You will need to enlist help for most of these tests. Perhaps work with another clairvoyant friend and test each other.

Write numbers one to twenty-five in black ink on small square white cards you cannot see through. Shuffle the cards and arrange them face down in four rows of six with a single extra card at the top.

Start at the top and hold a pendulum inside a large wide glass over each card in turn. You should hold the pendulum with the hand you write with and the glass in the other so that the pendulum is not touching the sides or bottom of the glass and half the pendulum chain is outside the glass. Ask the pendulum aloud to ring against the side of the glass the same number of times as the number on the chosen card. Move top to bottom, left to right. Write on a sheet of paper 'Card 1, 3 rings' and so on before going on to the next card.

Continue moving down each row, horizontally left to right

across the whole row before proceeding to the next and repeat the process. Do not worry if the pendulum gives the same answer for two cards as no one could get them all right. Afterwards check how many were right. You should expect to get five right by chance. Nine would be what is called a statistically significant result, above which something is happening psychically. Most clairvoyants of moderate to good ability might get between ten and fifteen right and more than that means you are moving into very evolved psychic energies indeed. Twenty out of twenty-five would be spectacular.

Ask a friend to sit in front of a computer on which there is a photograph of you open on one window (or use a photo of one of your children, a partner or a favourite pet: anything that has an emotional connection with you). In a second window, open a picture of something you dislike or fear. The emotional connection with both images should be with you. You should not be able to see the computer, if possible go into another room.

Ask the friend to display one of the images every minute and leave it on for about a minute before changing it to the next. Have either a stop watch or a clock with seconds and synchronise your start time (this is important to be totally accurate). Every minute you should *feel* rather than see your emotion to whatever is on the screen and before the end of the minute write your answer. Repeat for twenty-five images in total and then after a break, if you wish repeat for a further twenty-five. Measure your accuracy.

Make yourself a pack of five identical cards of each of five different designs. You can put any simple design you wish on the cards such as five different animals, fruits, shapes, modes of transport or household items. Each design must be distinct, a line drawing and in only one colour. The colours should be different for each. If you like, you can copy the shapes below to make a card pack of twenty-five cards in total, five of each, small enough to handle easily.

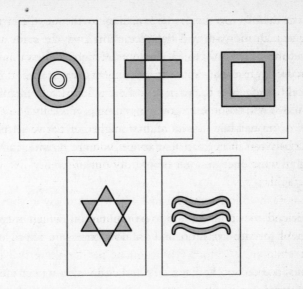

Carry out this test alone and repeat in batches of twenty-five, up to 150 guesses in total (six sequences in all).

Shuffle the cards well and put in a pile face down. Before dealing the top card focus on it, touch it and say aloud what it is. Look at the card after guessing and mark your answer on paper as either a tick or cross. Put the card back in the pack, reshuffle and repeat until you have twenty-five ticks or crosses. Five correct would be chance as before.

Guesses	Chance Score	Significant Score
25	5	9
50	10	16
75	15	22
100	20	28
125	25	34
150	50	63

Now try the same game with first a pack of seventy-eight tarot cards and then fifty-two playing cards.

Repeat the experiment exactly for fifty guesses, regardless of the number of cards in total to choose from, again returning the card after looking at it to the pack and reshuffling. Then try the same experiment, but this time as you touch the top card, do not guess its identity but that of the card beneath it (predicting two cards ahead). Check this second card, return to the pack and reshuffle for your fifty guesses or, if you are enthusiastic, keep going in multiples of twenty-five guesses up to 150. You will note the more the total guesses the wider the gap becomes between chance and significance and so be pleased at anything over significance once you get beyond fifty guesses.

Using a coin, hold it in cupped hands and wish strongly in your mind and visualise either heads or tails to be uppermost. Try either twenty-five, fifty or seventy-five times and see how often you are right.

Now use an ordinary six-sided dice and again wish strongly for one of the possible numbers to appear. When you have tried twenty-five times and recorded your results, add first an extra dice for the next twenty-five turns then three dices for the third twenty-five. Remember you are not predicting but using psychokinesis, or mind power, to affect the role of the dice or flip of the coin and so every correct answer over chance should be regarded as successful. When using two dice you can predict 1–12 (two times six) and for three dice 1–18 (three times six).

IF YOU DO NOT RESPOND WELL TO TESTS

Succeeding in psychic tests is not a requirement to be a good clairvoyant. Many people, myself included, operate best in real situations with real needs and people who have problems to be solved or decisions to be made. The following are, however, ways you can challenge yourself psychically and fine-tune your psychic gifts.

✧ Imagine the aura around crystals, plants and flames in terms of animate nature spirits. Even if you do not believe in nature spirits as such, describe what you feel when you touch or hold your hand over each as if they were spirit beings. That way you are able to externalise and express quite subtle energy differences clearly and creatively. This psychic discrimination is one of the greatest abilities in any form of psychic work and I would suggest even those of you who do the more formal tests try these exercises for fun.

✧ Crystals are the easiest natural substance to start with as their energies are quite clear and powerful even in a small stone. They are sometimes said to contain their own individual spirit guardians. If you do not have many crystals you can go into a crystal or New Age store and hold your curved fingertips and hands over some or, if you prefer, make hand contact with various stones and define how each feels like or unlike another, as though each had a separate guardian spirit.

✧ Try describing, in terms of nature spirit beings, an amethyst or citrine geode energy, a clear quartz crystal sphere, a small round rutilated or smoky quartz, a black obsidian arrow or pointed obsidian crystal, an opaque calcite pyramid, a creamy moonstone or shimmering white selenite, and a fossil. Alternatively choose seven different crystals you would like to work with. For example, a moonstone might be perceived as an ethereal white fairy with transparent wings of moonbeams. In contrast, a fossil could represent a very old wise gnarled brown earth spirit.

✧ As you get more experienced, work to differentiate crystals that differ only by shape and texture such as a chunk of unpolished pink rose quartz, a semi transparent rose quartz sphere and a rose quartz heart-shaped pendant, or an amethyst point and an amethyst pyramid.

✧ Progress to different fragrances as lighted incense such as lemongrass, orange, rose, rosemary, frankincense, lavender and pine, and explore the less definable but real energy differences between burning a rose essential oil, rose incense and smelling dried rose petals from fragrant growing roses.

❖ Fire also has its subtleties; the flame of a scented candle, an ordinary household dinner candle, a church or votive flame, natural beeswax or pure vegetable wax. Identify these as fiery nature beings and then experiment with the variations between different coloured candles.

❖ Describe the distinctions between healthy growing herbs or flowers in a garden, plants in a forest or near water, a healthy indoor pot plant, one that has been neglected, even a plastic plant that has a weak aura. What nature beings would each be manifest as?

❖ There is no limit to the energies you can compare: different kinds of water from the sea to waterfalls or an indoor water feature.

❖ Work also with sacred spirits and guardians by touching stones at sacred sites including, at various times, pre-Christian stone circles, stones on the external walls of Hindu or Oriental temples, synagogues, cathedrals and mosques. How do the sacred spirits of holy buildings differ from those of sacred wells, old stone circles, sacred trees, monoliths such as the Australian Aboriginal sacred mound Uluru, and stone or metal statues of deities, rock paintings or natural sculptures that are found throughout the world? Do any of these evoke memories of former lives? The sacred spirits are an ongoing project so keep meticulous detailed notes so you can make comparisons.

❖ When you have built up a collection of many different natural energies, check in books about nature spirits, beings and fairies and you may discover you have identified a fey form that has been described in other ages and cultures.

WHERE NEXT?

There are few limits to your own spiritual development. You can take further courses in aspects of psychic work that interest you, or undertake more formal training in healing therapies, mediumship, learn new divinatory arts or take a college degree in the spiritual arts or alternative religions. In time you may yourself teach courses, write books or found a healing centre. You can send off your showreels to television stations, set up your own psychic fairs or maybe choose to use your gifts to enrich your own life or that of friends or family and send healing into the world. Some of you will aspire to greatness, for as with any creative gift, such as music, most people can become good competent musicians who give pleasure to others as well as themselves. Just a select few go on to be great concert pianists.

But we all have spiritual potential that will grow through the years and with practice and use in the service of others. Part of the ability is an innate sense to finding the right path to our personal fulfilment if we trust our own wisdom. You can ask the cosmos for what you need and you can empower yourself into bringing those wishes into actuality. Always remember to pay the cosmos back for blessings whenever you can, in good deeds and kindness to others. The future is yours to make, so make it in the likeness of your own beautiful and unique vision.

Cassandra
October 2007

Useful Reading

Angels

Davidson, Gustav, *A Dictionary of Angels*, London, UK, Simon and Schuster, 1994

Eason, Cassandra, *Touched by Angels*, Quantum/Foulsham, 2006

Newcomb, Jacky, *An Angel Treasury*, Element/Thorsons, 2004

Parisen, Maria, *Angels and Mortals, Their Co-Creative Power*, Quest Books, 1994

Animal Wisdom

Eason, Cassandra, *The Psychic Power of Animals, how to communicate with your pet*, Piatkus, 2005

Palmer, Dawn Jessica, *Animal Wisdom*, Element, 2001

Sheldrake, Rupert, *Dogs That Know When Their Owners Are Coming Home – and other unexplained powers of animals*, California, Three Rivers Press, 2000

Smith, Penelope, *When Animals Speak: Advanced Interspecies Communication*, Oklahoma, Council Oak Books, 2004

Auras and Chakras

Davis, Brenda, *The Seven Healing Chakras: Unlocking Your Body's Energy Centers*, Berkeley CA, Ulysses Press, 2000

Eason, Cassandra, *Aura Reading*, London, UK, Piatkus Books, 2000

Eason, Cassandra, *Chakra Power*, Quantum/Foulsham, 2001

Karagulla, Shafica and Van Gelder Kunz, Dora, *The Chakras and the Human Energy Fields*, Theosophical University Press, 1994

Klotsche, Charles, *Color Medicine: The Secrets of Color/Vibrational Healing*, Arizona, Light Technology Publications, 1993

Sun, Howard and Dorothy, *Colour Your Life: Discover Your True Personality Through the Colour Reflection Reading*, Piatkus, 1999

Candles, Herbs, Oils and Incenses

Cunningham, Scott, *Complete Book of Incense, Oils and Brews,* St Paul, MN, Llewellyn, 2004

Cunningham, Scott, *Cunningham's Encyclopedia of Magical Herbs*, St Paul, MN, Llewellyn Publications, 1997

Eason, Cassandra, *Candle Power*, New York, Sterling, 2000

Eason, Cassandra, *Fragrant Magic*, Quantum/Foulsham, 2004

Higley, Connie and Alan, and Leatham, Pat, *Aromatherapy A to Z*, Hay House, 2002

Vickery, Roy, *A Dictionary of Plant-Lore*, Oxford University Press, 1995

Whitaker, Charlene, *Candles, Meditation and Healing,* St Paul, MN, Llewellyn, 2000

Crystals and Scrying

Andrews, Ted, *Crystal Balls and Crystal Bowls: Tools for Ancient Scrying and Modern Seership*, St Paul, MN, Llewellyn Publications, 1995

Cunningham, Scott, *Encyclopedia of Crystal, Gem and Metal Magic*, St Paul, MN, Llewellyn Publications, 1991

Eason, Cassandra, *The Illustrated Directory of Healing Crystals*, London, UK, Collins and Brown, 2004

Eason, Cassandra, *Scrying the Secrets of the Future*, New Jersey, New Page/Career Press, 2006

Gienger, Michael and Astrid, Mick, *Crystal Power, Crystal Healing: The Complete Handbook*, Cassell Illustrated, 1998

Divination Systems

Eason, Cassandra, *A Complete Guide to Divination,* Piatkus, 2004

Eason, Cassandra, *A Complete Book of Tarot*, Piatkus, 1999

Eason, Cassandra, *The Modern Day Druidess*, Piatkus, 2003 (for tree staves)

Mountfort, Paul Rhys, *Ogan, The Celtic Oracle of the Trees, Understanding, Casting and Interpreting the Ancient Druidic Alphabet*, Vermont, Destiny Books, 2002

Pollack, Rachel, *Seventy Eight Degrees of Wisdom, A Book of Tarot*, Thorsons, 1997

Thorsson, Edred, *Runecaster's Handbook, The Well of Wyrd*, Maine, Red Wheel/Weiser, 1999

Ghosts and the Paranormal

Auerbach, Loyd, *Hauntings and Poltergeists, A Ghost Hunter's Guide*, California, Ronin Publishing, 2004

Blum, Deborah, *Ghost Hunters: William James and the Search for Scientific Proof of Life After Death*, Arrow Books, 2007

Charles, Keith and Shuff, Derek, *Psychic Detective*, Blake Publishing, 2000

Morris, Richard, *Harry Price, the Psychic Detective*, Sutton Publishing, 2006

Nesbitt, Mark V., *Ghosts of Gettysburg: Spirits, Apparitions and Haunted Places of the Battlefield*, Pennsylvania Thomas Publications, 1991, also the subsequent volumes 2–5

Healing

Angelo, Jack, *Your Healing Power: A comprehensive guide to chanelling your healing energies*, Piatkus, 1998

Kavasch, E. Barrie and Baar, Karen, *American Indian Healing Arts: Herbs, Rituals, and Remedies for Every Season of Life*, Thorsons/Bantam US, 1999

Simpson, Liz, *The Healing Energies of Earth*, Gaia Books, 2005

Nature Spirituality

Cooper, Joe, *The Case of the Cottingley Fairies*, New York, Pocket Books, 1998

Devereux, Paul, *The Sacred Place, The Ancient Origin of Holy and Mystical Sites*, Cassell Illustrated, 2000

Eason, Cassandra, *A Complete Guide to Fairies and Magical Beings*, Piatkus, 2002

Froud, Brian, *Good Faeries, Bad Faeries*, Simon and Schuster, 1998

Hawkins, Jaq D., *Spirits of the Water*, Capall Bann, 2000

Past Lives and Reincarnation

Browne, Sylvia, *Past Lives, Future Healing, A Psychic Reveals The Secrets to Good Health and Great Relationships*, Piatkus, 2006

Eason, Cassandra, *Discover Your Past Lives*, Foulsham, 2005

Kubler-Ross, Elisabeth and Hardo, Trutz, *Children Who Have Lived Before: Reincarnation Today*, Rider and Co, 2005

Psychic Powers and Spiritual Development

Brennan, James H., *The Astral Projection Workbook: How To Achieve Out-of-Body Experiences*, New York, Sterling, 1990

Chiazzari, Suzy, *Flower Readings: Discover your true self with flowers through the ancient art of Flower Psychometry*, C W Daniel, 2000

Eason, Cassandra, *A Complete Guide to Psychic Development*, Piatkus, 2002

Eason, Cassandra, *10 Steps to Psychic Power*, 2002

Eason, Cassandra, *Pendulum Dowsing*, Piatkus, 2004

Farrell, Nick, *Magical Pathworking, Techniques of Active Imagination*, Llewellyn, 2003

Lonegren, Sig, *Spiritual Dowsing*, Gothic Images, 1986

Weiss, Brian L, *Meditation, Achieving Inner Peace and Tranquility in Your Life*, New York: Hay House, 2002

Psychic Protection

Eason, Cassandra, *Psychic Protection lifts the Spirit*, Quantum/Foulsham, 2001

Harbour, Dorothy, *Energy Vampires: A Practical Guide for Psychic Self-Protection,* Inner Traditions Bear and Company, 2003

Kingston, Karen, *Clear your Clutter with Feng Shui*, Piatkus, 2000

Matthews, Caitlin, *The Psychic Protection Handbook: Powerful Protection for Uncertain Times*, Piatkus 2005

Mickaharic, Draja, *Spiritual Cleansing, a Handbook of Psychic Self-Protection*, Maine, Red Wheel/Weiser, 2003

Psychic Tests

Blackmore, Susan J. and Hart-Davis, Adam, *Test your Psychic Powers: Find out the truth for yourself*, Harper Collins, 1995

Eysenck, H. J. and Sargent, Carl, *Are you Psychic?: tests and games to measure your powers*, Priori Books, 1996

Spiritualism, Mediumship and Spirit Guides

Cook, Grace and White Eagle, *The Quiet Mind, Sayings of White Eagle*, White Eagle Publishing Trust, 1983

DuBois, Alison, *We are their Heaven: Why the Dead Never Leave Us*, New York, Simon and Schuster Inc, 2006

Lodge, Sir Oliver, *Raymond Or Life And Death*, Montana, R E Kessinger Publishing Co, 1998

Ortzen, Tony, *Silver Birch, The Spirit Speaks*, Psychic Press, 1998

Roman, Sanaya and Packer, Duane, *Opening to Channel: How To Connect With Your Guides*, California, H J Kramer, 1989

Useful Contacts

CRYSTAL SUPPLIERS
I have only listed three suppliers I can recommend from personal experience. They all ship worldwide.

Bokförlaget New Page AB (Sweden)
High quality, wide ranging and unusual crystals plus Ancient Egyptian and authentically reproduced Viking artefacts from the local blacksmith
www.newpage.se

Charlie's Rock Shop (UK)
For high quality, reasonably priced fossils, crystals, geodes, pendulums, angels, power animals, crystal spheres and authentic Navajo jewellery
www.charliesrockshop.com

Isis Crystals (UK)
Wide range and high quality crystals, spheres, pendulums, geodes, angels, individual crystal treasures, power animals and other authentic Native North American artefacts
www.isis-crystals.com

GHOSTS
Australian Ghost Hunters Society
Extensive site listing Australia's most haunted sites, photographs, tips, articles and contacts
www.castleofspirits.com/Australianghosthunters

Gettysburg ghosts
For information and activities about America's Gettysburg, one of the world's most haunted areas
www.ghostsofgettysburg.com

The Ghost Club
UK-based and oldest ghost club in the world
www.ghostclub.org.uk

The International Ghost Hunters Society
Large Internet ghost investigation site with articles, photographs etc, US-based
www.ghostweb.com

HEALING
The National Federation of Spiritual Healers
Offers training as well as access to healers in UK. Also training courses contactable through this site in Australia, Canada, Germany, Ireland, Japan, New Zealand, Poland, Spain, Switzerland and the US
www.nfsh.org.uk

Rowancraft
For healing and training in Reiki and shamanic practices under the gentle guidance of Jane Rowan and Robin Oak
www.rowancraft.co.uk

MUSIC, MEDITATION, FEY MUSIC AND WORKSHOP CDS
Paradise Music
US and South America
www.paradisemusic.us.com

UK and Europe
www.paradisemusic.co.uk

MEDIUMSHIP AND SPIRITUALISM
The Arthur Findlay College (UK)
Incorporating the Spiritualist Lyceum Union
For courses, information and literature on spirit guides and all aspects
of mediumship and spiritualism
www.arthurfindlaycollege.org

Australian Spiritualist Association
Central contact point for mediumship and spiritualism in Australia
www.spiritualist.asn.au

National Spiritualist Association of Churches
American central contact for information on spiritualism and spiritualist churches
www.nsac.org

Psychic News online forum for mediums and psychics and all who are interested, details of classes etc in UK
www.psychicnews.org

Two Worlds Spiritual magazine
An excellent source of information and contacts, UK and beyond
www.users.globalnet.co.uk/~tortzen

Neopagan contacts
Pagan Awareness Network, Australia
Provides useful information and contacts for individuals and groups
within the pagan community
www.paganawareness.net.au

Pagan Federation International
Connections in the US and with other pagans worldwide
www.us.paganfederation.org

Pagan Federation UK

UK and international information and contacts for pagan individuals and groups. A good starting point

www.paganfed.org

Psychic development training
College of Psychic Studies

Investigation of psychic phenomena, classes, lectures etc in London

www.collegeofpsychicstudies.co.uk

SPIRITUALITY
Spheres magazine

A very useful high quality journal for the Southern Hemisphere and beyond on all matters spiritual, useful contacts, articles, details of practitioners and events

www.spiritguide.com.au

Web design advice for spiritual sites

This designer has an extensive spiritual background and the prices are very reasonable for high quality work to either set up or manage a site

Abi is an English web designer and graphic artist based in France

www.central- france.com/abi

Email with enquiries or an informal chat: abi@central-france.com

Cassandra Eason can be contacted for information about clairvoyance and spirituality as well as for details of courses, and she or her team will answer any questions you may have.

www.cassandraeason.co.uk

Index